# Resu[rrection] From Plato's Cave

Pete Delmonico &
Virginia Nodhturft

outskirts
press

Resurrected From Plato's Cave
All Rights Reserved.
Copyright © 2019 Pete Delmonico & Virginia Nodhturft
v2.0

The opinions expressed in this manuscript are solely the opinions of the author and do not represent the opinions or thoughts of the publisher. The author has represented and warranted full ownership and/or legal right to publish all the materials in this book.

This book may not be reproduced, transmitted, or stored in whole or in part by any means, including graphic, electronic, or mechanical without the express written consent of the publisher except in the case of brief quotations embodied in critical articles and reviews.

Outskirts Press, Inc.
http://www.outskirtspress.com

ISBN: 978-1-9772-3640-1

Cover image by Larry Capehart. All rights reserved - used with permission.

Outskirts Press and the "OP" logo are trademarks belonging to Outskirts Press, Inc.

PRINTED IN THE UNITED STATES OF AMERICA

# Table of Contents

| | |
|---|---|
| Dedication | i |
| Introduction | iii |
| Introduction to Plato's Allegory of the Cave | v |
| Foreword | vii |
| Learn How the Authors Met | ix |
| Acknowledgments | xi |
| | |
| 1: Emotional Scars: Living in a House of Horror Childhood Days | 1 |
| 2: Breaking the Cycle of Abuse | 31 |
| 3: Unexpected Tragedy Hits | 49 |
| 4: Failed Attempt to Escape Bonds of Guilt & Anger | 61 |
| 5: Ditching the Chains, Demons and Enemies | 71 |
| 6: Bringing Joy, Happiness and Peace Back to the Heart | 85 |
| 7: Unleashed Emotional Chains | 88 |
| 8: Poems Depicting How Jack Felt In and Out of the Cave | 104 |
| 9: The Mighty Hero Becomes A Miracle | 113 |
| 10: The Coronavirus Hits the World… | 123 |
| 11: Key Lessons for America from the Pandemic | 152 |
| 12: Ann is Now in Heaven | 171 |
| 13: Jack Faced with Creating a New Life | 179 |
| 14: Lessons Learned from Jack | 188 |
| | |
| Appendix A: Enrichment Reading | 195 |
| About the Authors | 200 |

# Dedication

**First, this book** is dedicated to Jack Long for his extraordinary ability to cope with brutal adverse circumstances. First, living in a household with an alcoholic father and domestic violence, then coping with the tragic stroke of his beloved wife. The lifelong suffering, he endured and his ability to overcome it all is an inspiration to all who read his story.

Secondly, the book is dedicated to **Coach Rocco Polo** for mentoring, guiding, and serving as Jack's surrogate father. Coach Polo developed aspects of Jack's character that helped Jack overcome the cycle of abuse that he experienced as a child. Jack embraced the values of hard work, perseverance, never giving up, teamwork and commitment that took a stronghold on Jack as he faced moral, ethical, spiritual, work challenges that the good life presents.

Lastly, this book is dedicated to **Joel Osteen** for his books that helped Jack undo the chains of anger, guilt, anxiety, loneliness, and depression enabling Jack to take back his life after his beloved wife had a stroke. Joel Osteen's guidance helped Jack to delete negative thoughts of financial hardships, guilt, anger, depression, and loneliness that enabled him to resurrect from Plato's Cave and be a better support to his wife.

# Introduction

**This is a** story about a man named Jack Long who struggled against unsurmountable odds his entire life. The book is actually two stories of profound adversity that Jack endured but survived in a thriving manner—1) how Jack grew up in an abusive dysfunctional family in the era of the 50's and broke the cycle of abuse, and 2) how Jack overcame severe overpowering, prolonged grief when his wife sustained a stroke.

The story shares how Jack was successful in breaking the cycle of abuse with the help of his high school coach and went on to become a loving warm father and a faithful, devoted husband. Jack had the intelligence, insight, inspiration, and commitment to break the cycle of abuse that he experienced in his dysfunctional family.

The story continues to share extraordinary efforts Jack made to come out of Plato's cave cocooned and chained inside suffering with extreme grief after his beloved wife had a severe stroke. It describes with the help of Joel Osteen's books how Jack developed the courage to overcome and escape from the bonds of loneliness, anxiety, and guilt he felt after his wife fell ill just before retirement. He overcame with much difficulty the prolonged grief lasting seven years while chained in the cave. He finally created a new fulfilling life abundant with joy, happiness, and peace. When he took back his life, he became a better support to his wife on his daily visits to the nursing home by being more vibrant, joyful, and interesting.

Indeed, the heartache he endured as a child and when his wife fell ill was extraordinary. His strong character and faith served him well in overcoming the brutal hardships, difficulties, and suffering. He has a warm heart filled with love, ears that listen and a hand that's always willing to help. He has a can-do attitude and a never give up character trait.

This is an extraordinary story of how Jack triumphed over severe suffering with dignity, passion, and pride as he opened his heart to change to bring peace and joy to his heart. His ability to develop coping skills and triumph over sustained abuse and chaos of his life was remarkable. This book should encourage others who are struggling with the same sorrow that Jack lived through.

Pete Delmonico and Virginia Nodhturft

# Introduction to Plato's Allegory of the Cave

**Plato's Allegory of** Cave is a story about three prisoners in cave tied to stone forcing them to look at a one wall in the cave. They were prisoners since childhood. Behind them was the opening to the cave and the only reality they experienced were the shadows that were cast on the wall that they were forced to look at. Men walked by with stones, animals and other items casting shadows on the wall. This was what they perceived as reality. They played games predicting what the next shadow would be and the one that guessed correctly was looked at as the master. They had no awareness or knowledge that there was a whole world outside the cave with lakes, waterfalls, flowers, trees, clouds, stars, moon, and the sun.

One day one prisoner escaped and could not believe his eyes. He saw the sun for first time. He saw trees and beautiful flowers and thought this is not real. He looked up at the moon at nighttime and saw the twinkling stars in the sky and was overwhelmed with the beauty. Over time he realized that it was real and what was in the cave was not real. He went back to tell the other prisoners what he found and tried to release them, but they got angry and did not believe him. They refused to leave what they perceived as comfort and their reality.

The escaped prisoner experienced joy, happiness and regained his thoughts about the true meaning of his life. The escaped prisoner had a whole new outlook on life and experienced a sense of joy that made him vibrant, exciting, and happy. He became creative, self-confident, and moved on to another chapter in his life.

Jack was trapped in Plato's Cave and like the one prisoner who escaped. And like the escaped prisoner Jack also escaped the cave, took back his life and became a free person once again. He too became creative, self-confident, and was able to experience once again joy, and happiness. Jack finally was able to move on to another chapter in his life too.

# Foreword

**In Plato's cave,** our protagonist sees only the shadows on the back wall and believes that to be the entirety of all existence, unable to see the great wide world of color and motion that is happening all around him. That is Jack's existence as he struggles with his childhood of abuse and violence at the hands of a sadistic father. For years he believes that his reality is all there can be. Then with the support and mentroing of a high school coach he begins to see a somewhat wider reality. Seeing the beauty in the world follows slowly as Jack begins to experience the joys of love with his wife Ann and with his son, Jack Junior. Then through a successful life of productive employment, Jack experiences the kind of fulfillment he could never have envisioned as a young boy.

As a young adult, Jack successfully emerged, fully resurrected, from his cave to enjoy life with his family. Ann was his always cheerful and loving support and Jack, Jr. his great joy. However, as age begins to affect Jack and Ann, they experience a catastrophic change when Ann has major health problems. Unable to care for his disabled wife, Jack has to relinquish his precious wife to a nursing home where he visits twice a day to share every meal with her. The loneliness and depression of Jack's youth returns as he envisions only a lonely future, with Ann no longer meeting him at the door and cooking favorite meals. He sees a future devoid of hope and joy. As we read, we wonder if Jack will successfully navigate this difficult time and develop the needed coping skills as he faces the final loss of Ann.

*Resurrected from Plato's Cave,* as the title suggests, is a book about triumphing over adversity that can be a model of hope for so many others who experience the same difficulties as young Jack, and also the same grief as mature Jack. This book should be an encouragement for others experiencing life's difficulties. Jack's faith in God is evident throughout this book; his solutions to his problems often depend on support from his God.

It is not surprising that Dr. Virginia Nodhturft would be co-author with Pete Delmonico, a childhood friend, on a book about grief and depression. Dr. Nodhturft has been a nurse for many years and had the opportunity to see many in the throes of life's challenges. Dr. Nodhturft and I have been long time nursing colleagues. Now that we have both retired, I admire her productivity as she writes her second book. Her first was researched for a decade and provided a different perspective on the American Civil War. In it she describes the work of her ancestor who was a spy for the Union. Now she has turned her focus to a different type of battle.

When she showed me an early draft of some of the chapters of *Resurrected from Plato's Cave*, I was charmed and encouraged her to move ahead with completing the book and publishing it. Readers should be encouraged as they follow Jack's struggles to his ultimate successes.

*Susan C. McMillan, PhD, ARNP, FAAN*
Emeritus Distinguished Professor
University of South Florida

# LEARN HOW THE AUTHORS MET

**GINNY AND PETE** met in Elementary School Maybrook, New York in the third grade. They both went to High School in Maybrook, NY and graduated in the class of 1961. Ginny and Pete have been lifelong friends ever since meeting in school. Here they are in the ninth grade at the Junior Prom in Maybrook High School 1958. Ginny taught Pete how to dance and he invited her to the prom.

After many years Pete and Ginny reconnected by Coach Tony Gesso who was Pete's Varsity Basketball Coach and Ginny's CYO Girls Basketball Coach. Both Ginny and Pete feel it was a divine intervention that Coach Gesso brought them together to write this book about a mutual friend to help other people cope with the adversity that their dear friend Jack Long endured for many years.

Ginny and Pete both met their spouses in high school. Pete married Shirley Bidosky and they have been married for 55 years. Ginny married Phil Nodhturft, Jr. and has been married for 50 years.

Pete and Shirley had one son, Pete, Jr. who married a woman named Margo Pappova. Pete, Jr. is a highly successful businessman who lives in California.

Ginny and Phil, Jr had one son, Philip, III who married Melissa Jill Knight. They are both practicing attorneys in the Tampa Bay Area and live in South Tampa.

# Acknowledgments

**Valerie Kelleher** a work colleague and friend is recognized for her invaluable assistance in the technical formatting of the book. Her dedicated enthusiastic creative talent was a huge help to us in writing the book. She was very generous in sharing her time, support, interest, and expertise. We could not have crossed the finish line without your expertise Valerie! We are eternally grateful to you for all your assistance.

**Katie Rooney, RN Psychiatric Nurse** Ginny's lifelong friend is being recognized for her expert insight and feedback on the book. Her suggestions were extraordinarily helpful to us in preparing the manuscript. Katie your interest, support and direction were appreciated more than you know. Thank you, Katie!

**Stephanie Hoffman, Ph.D. Psychologist,** retired from The Department of Veterans Affairs and is currently **Professor of Psychology St. Leo College Tampa Florida,** a colleague and friend is being acknowledged for her clinical expertise and feedback provided to the authors. Her sageness, perceptiveness and clear sightedness was extremely helpful and appreciated by the authors. Thank you, Stephanie!

**Susan McMillan, Ph.D., ARNP, FAAN, Emeritus Distinguished Professor University of South Florida College of Nursing** a colleague and friend is being acknowledged for her perception, wisdom, superb feedback that was exceptionally valuable to the authors. Susan's expertise and research publications in the area of caregivers were extrordinary and helped the authors to strengthen the manuscript. Thank you, Susan!

Gratitude is extended to **Dana Nelson**, Author Representative for Outskirts Press for all the help she provided to us during the publishing process. She was there for us from day one till the very end, guiding, mentoring and supporting the authors. Dana has an extraordinary virtue for patience. Thank you, Dana.,

**Eve Bidosky** is being recognized for her support of the two authors and her patience and expertise in helping us to format Pete's sketch. Her help and feedback were invaluable. Eve's interest in our project and encouragement to proceed was heartwarming. You're the greatest inspiration to both of us. Thank you, Eve!

**Phil Nodhturft, Jr.** is being recognized for helping the authors edit various chapters and for his warm loving support and assistance in writing the book. His consultation during the writing process was appreciated and valued. His encouragement to keep going with the book was inspiring to the authors. Thank you, Phil!

**Coach Tony Gesso** is recognized for being a source of inspiration to both Pete and Ginny. He developed aspects of their character such as hard work, perseverance, accepting losses with grace, teamwork, respect for others, and a never give up attitude, that carried us both through life as they faced moral, ethical, academic and career challenges that the life presents. He brought Ginny and Pete together after many years, by passing on to Pete that Ginny was asking about how he was doing, and Pete asked for her telephone number that Coach Gesso had on his phone. Thus, the reunion took place and the book was born to hopefully help others in similar situations. Thank you, Tony Gesso you're the greatest!!

**Joel Osteen, Author of** *Your Best Life Now, The Power of I Am, Think Better Live Better and You Can and You Will* is being acknowledged for the extraordinary inspiration Jack received from these books so he could experience the full potential that God intended him to have. Joel Osteen's remarkable insights and encouragement throughout his books have led Jack to unleash his emotional chains and find purpose, and vison to reach his full potential. He moved from bitterness, anger, anxiety, guilt, and fear to feeling victorious, strong, positive, and self-confident. Thank you, Joel!

**Marc D. Sanders,** songwriter of *I Hope You Dance* is being recognized for his kind permission to print the lyrics of the song ***I Hope You Dance***. This song was dedicated to Jack Long for the remarkable ability to break the cycle of abuse in his family and for his exceptional hard work of taking his life back from a period of prolonged grief after his wife suffered a stroke. Thank you, Marc, for your support.

**Igor Lacertis** appreciation is extended to Igor Http://www.lacertisphoto.com who took our head shot photos. He's the best photographer in the Hudson Valley Area, New York. Not only is he incredibly talented he makes the session fun. Thanks, Igor for a great time. If in need of photos for your special occasion wedding, anniversary, birthday. engagement, birth, reunion call 845-978-2613

Accolades are extended to **Phillip Schuster**, On Trak Promographics, Inc 6610E. Fowler Avenue, Suite F Temple Terrace, Fl 33617 813-988-7228 for helping the authors format the images during the printing process. His upbeat, positive, helpful demeanor and technology expertise was invaluable. He is the best printing, image design company in the Tampa Bay Area. Thank you, Phillip,!

**Larry Capehart** is recognized for completing the front book cover photo. Larry is a talented art teacher in the Pasco County School District. His enthusiasm encouraged the authors to continue with the book. Thank you, Larry, for your extraordinary sketch. Your hard work, interest and time was appreciated. You're the best Larry!

# 1

# Emotional Scars: Living in a House of Horror Childhood Days

**This narrative of** Jack Long's life begins when Jack was a young boy in elementary school in the 1950's. Each day he came home to a household with an alcoholic father and extraordinary abuse. It was an era when domestic violence was not discussed with anyone outside the family not friends, neighbors, teacher, counselors, or priests. It was considered taboo in that era to let anyone know of the horror that took place within the household. The family was filled with shame, guilt and fear and all secrets were kept among themselves.

Moreover, teachers, counselors, coaches, and clergy were not educated and did not have the skills to manage domestic violence. Even if these professionals were aware that a family was suffering under those circumstances, they turned a blind eye to it. They thought the proper thing to do was not get involved in the family's business.

In fact, this cultural era did not have societal resources in place.

Domestic violence crisis hot lines, shelters or other societal, community agencies to help families facing the hardships and torment experienced from domestic violence were not yet part of the American popular culture.

Thus, the stigma attached to having an alcoholic parent resulting in domestic violence was so forbidding in that era. This coupled with the fact that there was a lack of helpful resources available to families victimized by alcoholic spouses and a lack of trained teachers and clergy to help families helps explains why the children and wife did not seek help from teachers, counselors, clergy or community organizations.

Explicitly, Jack Long was the oldest child of five children. He had two brothers and two sisters. Jack grew up in a dysfunctional family with a violent alcoholic father. His father created an abusive household environment filled with fear and chaos.

When his father came home, Jack felt overwhelming panic and was terrified that his father would either hurt him physically or batter his mother. He lay in bed feeling anxiety as he waited for the verbal and physical abuse to start. His father's loud boisterous voice yelling at his mother sent tremors down his spine.

As his father's voice gets louder and more violent in tone his stomach starts to roil. He rises from his bed to check on his mom to make sure she's OK. He looks at his father's swollen red face, bloodshot eyes, and disheveled hair. He smells the alcohol, cigarette combo, repulsive buffalo breath as his father is yelling unmercifully at his mother. His presence annoys his father and he threatens to make him suffer with significant injury if he did not go back to bed. His mother pleads with him to go back to bed for fear her husband may follow through on his threat. Jack retreats to the bedroom slowly and reluctantly.

Finally, the yelling stops and by now because his father passes out on the floor in a total drunken stupor. Jack is so pumped up with adrenaline he cannot sleep and gets up in the morning to go to school feeling unrefreshed.

Expressly, one night when his father opened the door to the house, he was a madman, ranting and raving and picked up a butcher knife. He held the butcher knife against his mother as he was threatening to kill her. His voice sounded as if he was possessed. Hearing the commotion and the voice tempo building up to a shattering tone Jack jumped out of bed and ran in front of his mother and said if you kill her you will have to kill me first. The father looked Jack in his eyes with rage pouring out of every orifice and dropped the knife and walked away. His father abused his mother frequently both physically and emotionally. She was totally beaten down with no quality to her life. She lived in panic and trepidation every day of her life as a battered wife.

Despite being frightened for his life Jack, on many occasions he tried as a small boy to stand up to his father to protect his mother. He loved his mom abundantly and often was more fearful of her life being taken away than his own.

Frequently, his father not only verbally abused his wife on a continual basis, but verbally abused all the children as well. He yelled at the children, bullied them, and threatened physical harm to them. There were times when he became so violent his father whacked their buttocks when they did something wrong in the eyes of his father. It didn't take much to enrage his father. He had no impulse control.

Amazingly, the children developed creative strategies to lessen the pain when the beatings took place. For example, one of the children put a book in their underwear when he went to bed to lessen the pain from the whacking.

When the abuse took place each time Jack examined in his mind what if anything he did to contribute to the painful mistreatment from his father. He grew up in a constant state of guilt, thinking that maybe he was the cause of his father's abusive behavior. Maybe if I didn't ask for new sneakers or a new bike the abuse would not have happened. Thus, his whole life he asked for nothing and grew up with nothing. He didn't realize he had absolutely nothing to do with his father's raging states of mind.

Sadly, he longed for his father to tell him he loved him and wished he would show him just an ounce of respect with a little dignity. But it never came.

With attention to his father's behavior there was an occasion on a snowy bitter cold winter night his father with the whole family in the car stopped at a bar to get himself a drink. While he was drinking in the bar, he left the family in the car freezing to death with their teeth chattering and shivering. They put their hands under their armpits or in between the thighs to keep warm. He was in the bar for a long time. Jack's mom and siblings were in the car not only shivery, but tired and hungry as well.

Finally, Jack honked the horn for his father to come out. When he came out, he yelled and screamed at them in a savage manner for honking the horn. He was angered and his blood boiling with the honking of the car horn. Jack tensed himself for the blows that he expected, but they didn't come. His father returned to the bar and continued to drink.

After more time went by, Jack honked the horn again. When his father came out, he was like an enraged madman with all guns blazing. His face beet red and with his neck veins palpating, he asked "who the hell honked the horn". His mother spoke up quickly and said it was her, because she didn't want Jack to get a beating.

Once again, he sauntered back in the bar. After a very long time Jack's mother mounted her courage and decisively went in the establishment, grabbed 88 dollars off the bar and drove the car to the grocery store and bought food so the children could eat and then go to bed.

Particularly, his father had no concern for the fact that his wife had no food to feed the children and that it was getting late far past the children's bedtime. He had no regard for how his self-absorbed, unmindful selfish behavior impacted the children.

Indeed, a very intimidating fearful experience for Jack was the night the chief of police and all his deputies came knocking on the door looking for Jack's father to arrest him. Jack's father hadn't been home in three nights hiding from the police. Just seeing all those policemen with guns on their hips come barging in the home with stern looking faces was panic-stricken for Jack. The family explained they haven't seen him in three days and didn't know where he was located. The police left and the family never did learn why he was being arrested.

Surely, his father was a bully. He bullied everyone in the family, neighbors, and townspeople. Jack's father was also a womanizer and was found with all the promiscuous women in town. He frequented all the bars in town spending all the family's money. Sometimes he was involved in fist fights at the saloon, that resulted in extensive damage to the bar.

Notably, on one occasion in the evening a huge overweight man got in Jack's father's face and said, "You owe me money you son of bitch". His father became incensed. Infuriated, he fought with the man and began to knock holes in the walls and did other interior damage as well. The bartender threw both men out of the bar with the help of a huge bouncer.

Frequently, some of the men he fought with in the bar came knocking on the house door in the middle of the night looking for his father to knock the living daylights out of him. His father when liquored up was a total monster, mean and vicious. The children were paralyzed with fear, scared witless, shaking, and frightened to death.

Moreover, there were several occasions when Jack's father came home at three in the morning all boozed up with several other tanked up drunks. He dragged his wife out of bed and demanded that she cook for him and all the men. He felt entitled to "ownership rights" and treated his wife as if she were a slave to fulfill every single need of his. He owned his wife in his mind. He denigrated and terrorized her daily. If any of the men looked at his wife or if she looked at one of the men, he'd punch them to damnation. As his verbal demands for cooked food reached a high pitch, it created a commotion. This loud disorder woke up the children who had to go to school the next day. All this ruckus was spine chilling, fearsome and unnerving for the children and their mom.

Above all, on any given day Jack never knew what to expect when he came home from school. It produced unpredictable and uncontrollable stress for Jack. For example, he came home one day and opened the new convertible car his father just bought. When he opened the door a woman stone drunk was lying in the front seat totally incoherent. It was a shocking, ghastly sight.

Surely, this constant chaos led to emotional confusion, frequent nightmares, anxiety, crying and a feeling of helplessness. This unforeseeable environmental turmoil, nonstop arguments, inconsistency, and mayhem were rampant in the household when the children were in elementary school.

Without fail, his father constantly used fear techniques to control his children. When Jack was eight years old his father made him get in front of a twelve-year-old pitcher in Little League. Jack was petrified. Each attempt on Jack's part to retreat due to sheer fear was immediately met with angered resistance by his father. His father shamed him and forced him to stand in front of this pitcher as Jack shook in his boots in a state of panic.

Often when the children were with their father, he just left them in the car while he went into a bar or when he stopped off to an unknown house where he had a rendezvous with one of the vulnerable woman, that he charmed into sexual activities.

With this in mind, another time when Jack was around eight years old his father drove to a bar. He left him in the car by himself while his father went into the bar for a few drinks. After hours in the bar a complete stranger came out to the car and Jack was crying. He asked where his father was. The strange man said "You don't want to see your father right now. I'm going to take you home".

In this case, Jack's father got into a massive brawl inside the bar and got attacked and was beaten and lying on the floor. His father was pounded like a dandelion in a hailstorm. He was a sight. This whole scene was horrifying, fearsome and scary for Jack. He came to the bar with his father and left with a stranger, not knowing what happened to his father or what was going to happen to him.

To be sure, his father seemed to receive joy from scarring his children at every step of the way. It was a sadistic tendency he demonstrated frequently. Jack was about eight years old, and his father forced him to get on the Ferris Wheel at a local fair knowing full well he was scared to death of that ride. He got on the ride reluctantly begging his father to take him off. When the wheel got to the top the ride stopped and his father started swinging the chair back and forth vigorously. Jack broke down in tears begging his father to stop swinging the chair. He was in a panic state and his father just laughed and thought the whole thing was funny.

Still to this day Jack can't get on a Ferris Wheel. Flashbacks of the time when he was so frightened of the ride occur, making him feel very uneasy and feeling emotional turmoil within.

Here and there, as a young boy, Jack had odd jobs to make some spending money. He mowed lawns, shoveled snow, worked at the railroad refilling the ice in the cabooses and woke up the train crew and engineers in the local hotel to get the train to its next destination. His father showed up on each job and demanded all his money claiming the electricity would go off if he didn't hand over the money that Jack earned. He left Jack feeling hopeless, helpless, and with the belief that there was no way out.

Sadly, his father had countless lost jobs that didn't last long leaving his family in financial devastation. So, he rounded up multiple jobs here and there to make some money. Specifically, one job was working for a dry-cleaning store. He made Jack do his job which was to pass out flyers to all the houses outlining the dry-cleaning services. Then he told him pick up the dry cleaning to bring it to the dry-cleaning store. There was a mean dog on the grounds of one of the houses known to attack people. His father never extended the common courtesy to warn him about the danger he may encounter at that one house.

Markedly, his father was very bright, handsome, tall, had dark thick eyebrows and dark wavy hair. His upper arms revealed muscle definition and sinew. He was a snake charmer and the woman were attracted to him.

Thus, he used his physical attributes, intellect, and sweet-talking talent in his father's other new job. He was a door to door salesman selling household goods. The people bought the item and were permitted to pay for it on time schedule, so they didn't have to pay in full for it.

In particular, on this job, Jack's father made monthly rounds to pick up the money. On his rounds he met all the vulnerable, desperately lonely, needy women and on the trail. His psychopathic condition preyed on these women. He fed into their loneliness and told them how gorgeous and wonderful they were, making the woman feel special. He enticed the woman with his superficial charisma and calculated charm. He took advantage of the woman, deceived them, and had sexual relationships with all of them without any guilt or feelings of remorse. He left all his victims wounded and traumatized by his lack of decency and empathy. Once these women were no longer of any use to him, he discarded them like one would discard a dirty tissue.

Often, he'd bring Jack in the car and told him to play with the woman's children outside while he'd go in for his quick love making session. Jack began to have a pervasive feeling of uneasiness and began to suspect that something bad was going on inside that made him feel sad and uncomfortable.

In effect, his father's lack of empathy and cold heartedness was displayed on an evening when his father dropped Jack off outside a skating ring one bitter cold night. His father told him he'd be back shortly to pick him up. He went off to a bar and forgot all about Jack. He was horror struck wondering where his father was and was worried that the place would close before his father got there. He was sick with worry that he'd be all alone outside in the frigid cold freezing to death and not feeling very safe.

Finally, after four long hours his father showed up to pick him up. He had no regard for how fearful being left alone for four hours was for his son.

Over and over, Jack was left with broken promises and deceit that over time impacted his basic sense of trust. His trust was shaken not only in his father, but other people. After all, if you can't trust your father who can you trust was his thinking.

Sadly, one of his siblings wet the bed till he was 12 years old. Over time he started displaying verbal abuse to his mother. His brother was patterning his behavior after his father's. One time his mother was ironing his brother's shirts and one shirt had a wrinkle in it and his brother threw it on the floor chastising his mother for falling down on the job.

Additionally, his mother had to frequently wash the brother's bed sheets and his brother, once again showed displeasure with the washed sheets and verbally abused his mother. This upset Jack a lot. He went into the bedroom and said to his brother, "If you ever talk to mom like that again, you will live to regret it."

Unfortunately, this household chaos and bedlam took place daily and led to environmental confusion for all the children. They could not understand why all this pandemonium madness did not take place in friends' home. They longed to have a calm family life like their friends seemed to enjoy. They couldn't figure out why their life was so awful. They felt so alone and sad that they lived under these circumstances.

To enumerate, one of the brothers was out riding a bike and something got caught in the spoke of the wheel. He fell off the bike and severely injured his leg. He hobbled home and his mother took one look at it and put him in bed. He was unable to bear weight on the foot and it was beet red and swelled up like a balloon. The pain was unbearable. He missed three days of school.

Finally, his father came into the bedroom and kicked his leg and said, "get out of bed there's nothing wrong with your leg". The brother let out a blood curdling scream and his mother called their family doctor and he came immediately to the house. The doctor examined his leg and said to Jack's father "what the hell is wrong with you? Your son has a broken leg and needs to be in the hospital immediately".

Important to realize, this same younger brother started showing a pattern of abusive behavior from a young age. He threw coke bottles at Jack, he cut the heads of chickens off with a golf club, he threw his sister into a snow bank one night telling her she had to go out in the freezing cold to the store one block away and get him a snack. He did the same thing with his younger brother insisting he go to the store and get him a coke.

Moreover, he bossed everyone around and yelled at his siblings frequently if they didn't comply with his wishes. He slammed his sister against the wall one night and forbid her to go out if he didn't like her outfit. He was role modeling his father's abusive, disdainful, bullying behavior.

In those days, when the kids played basketball in the street or the YMCA, two boys had the privilege of choosing one by one the players on their team. Jack always had to pick his brother on his team because no one wanted him. He had difficulty developing relationships with others even at a noticeably young age. When Jack left home to live on his own his younger brother continued to abuse his sisters and younger brother.

To further enumerate, Jack's father abused his younger sister too. She was babysitting one time in the neighborhood. She asked her boyfriend to drop off some records for her to play while babysitting. The boyfriend and several of his buddies dropped off the records and left.

Somehow, Jack's father got word that several boys were at the door of the house where she was babysitting. He went over to the house barged inside in complete rage, inspected the entire house, and despite seeing no one, but the children she was babysitting, he dragged her out of the house by the hair called her awful names. He left the two toddlers completely alone with no supervision. She cried and begged him to let her go back to supervise the children. She was terrified that the children were left alone, and she was responsible for their welfare. After crying hysterically, he let her go back to the house. She was humiliated and hurt by the names he called her and felt so bad because of his lack of trust in her. It was a tormenting experience for her.

Another key point, Jack's father was always looking to take advantage of people to support his drinking addiction. One-night Jack's father brought home a monkey in a cage. He took it from some lady in town with the intention of selling it for liquor money. The monkey got out of the cage and bit everyone in sight. The monkey was vicious. The monkey defecated and voided all over and the house stunk to high heaven. He wasn't home most of the time and didn't give a damn that the monkey was a menace to all in the family.

However, the family had to put up with this monkey until he was able to sell it. They had to put the monkey outside due to the awful smell and kids and people from all over the town came by to see the monkey. It was quite an attraction for the townspeople. Finally, his father found some sucker that bought the monkey, and he never told the buyer what a vicious creature it was.

As if the bullying from Jack's father wasn't enough, he also suffered from sexual abuse from his young uncle. The uncle was tewlve and Jack was eight. Jack spent weekends at his uncle's house, and because they were so close in age, they had a great time. Jack looked up to his uncle and loved visiting him on weekends. One day, however, the uncle took Jack aside and tried to have oral sex with Jack. When Jack refused, the uncle told Jack to do it on him. Jack refused again and went into the house to get away from him.

The next day the uncle and Jack went to a neighbor's house. The neighbor was a friend of the uncle. The three of them, Jack, the uncle, and the uncle's friend were in a tent. Jack made believe he was sleeping because they were touching each other's private parts. The uncle gave the friend a blow job and then the friend gave the uncle one. All the while they thought Jack was sleeping. He felt extremely uncomfortable and had a sense that he was violated.

Additionally, the day after that took place the uncle was down in the basement of the house having sex with a twelve-year-old girl. He made Jack be the lookout for grandpa at the bottom of the steps. The girl was not forced to have sex; she seemed to enjoy it and Jack later thought of her as a bad girl. That was a weekend in hell.

To be sure, he never told his parents what happened that weekend, because he thought he would get in trouble and be blamed for the abuse. Or that they wouldn't believe him, and it would cause strife within his family and his uncle's family. He kept it a secret. He no longer went to the uncle's house. He gave his parents excuse after excuse why he didn't want to go. This whole scene at age eight scared him a lot. He had horrific nightmares for a long time. He also had mini panic attacks filled with anxiety that kept him awake at night.

All this fear, confusion, bewilderment, sadness and anger from this incident and the constant abuse from his father made Jack feel different from others and led to feeling insecure. The chronic anxiety and sense of insecurity led to social isolation. Jack found himself avoiding social activities as he struggled with psychological distress. He never felt like he fit in with his classmates.

Despite his insecurities when in seventh grade Jack had a crush on a Glens Falls girl Janice Swihart. He'd ride his bicycle to her house hoping to get a glimpse of her, but when he did see her, she wouldn't give him the time of day. This of course reinforced his feelings of insecurity, unworthiness and feeling he didn't fit in with his classmates.

## High School Days

When in high school Jack's father continued to verbally abuse him threatening to violently injure him if he ever got into trouble with the police or his teachers when he was living in the home. Jack was always afraid to engage in any mischievous behavior that his high school friends occasionally engaged in for fear of having to face his father. On one occasion his friends stole some playground equipment and he told them not to do it. He told them return the equipment or you're going to get into trouble.

Another time his friends went to the local Country Club after hours and they took the golf carts for a joy ride digging up and destroying the green and the carts they drove. The damage amounted to hundreds of dollars. The boys were caught, the police were called, and their parents had to repay the money for all the damages.

For fear that he'd get in trouble he never engaged in any of these activities. He was terrified that the police would catch him and then he'd have to deal with his father, a fate worse than death. With this in mind he was an obedient boy all through his school years with teachers. He never participated in any mischievous behavior in the town like his classmates.

To be sure, in high school Jack was blessed with handsome looks and extraordinary athletic talent. This made him extremely popular among the girls from the surrounding towns of Glen Falls in high school. He was completely oblivious to the fact that all the girls would give their right arm to have a date with him.

Truly, he never had any money or a car to take a girl out. This coupled with his feelings of insecurity, unworthiness and not fitting in resulted in him never asking anyone on a date. He became socially isolated.

But the girls found him and invited him on dates. The girls found someone who had a car and they asked him out on dates. He dated the hottest chicks in the surrounding towns, Christine Oakes, Nancy Nelson, Ann Marlow, and many others.

In fact, he lost his virginity in the back seat of a car to Christine Oakes. To be sure, he was aware that she had a reputation among the guys as being very promiscuous. The image she had was that she was easy to get to first base with.

Jack being the handsome athletic basketball star, it was not surprising, she sought Jack out. She was a cheerleader and he was the good-looking basketball star. She finally was successful in getting a date with Jack. They double dated and he found himself in the backseat of the car with her. She had been around the block a few times and guided him in the process of him losing his virginity.

Indeed, she was in high demand not only because she was promiscuous, but because she was beautiful. The ironic thing is that his dad was having an affair with her mother at the same time.

Then, Jack dated another girl named Kristy. As they started making out in the car, Kristy forcibly plunged her tongue down Jack's throat swirling it around and he said to himself "what the hell is she doing". He was shocked and scared. He never had a girl do that to him before. He was so grossed out. He later learned it was called a French Kiss. He was so turned off that was the first and last time he dated her.

Although he felt insecure around girls and never had any money or a car to take them out on a date, he did date quite a bit, because the girls always invited him to go out on double dates and to parties. He gained the reputation for being a hunk, completely unknown to him. He had no idea that's how the girls viewed him.

Not surprisingly, girls from all over were hot on the trail and made themselves available to him not only for dates, but for sexual intimacy. He had one rule before he engaged in sex. They had to reassure him that they were in that safe part of the menstrual cycle where they could not get pregnant. He was terrified of two things when having sex, namely contacting syphilis and pregnancy.

At long last, Jack finally got his driver's license and he was so pleased with himself for passing the test. One night his father got mad at him, took his driver's license, and tore it up so he couldn't go out that night. His mother pasted the license back for Jack and said, "Here I pasted your license together; go in the family car to where you were going, he won't be back for a while".

He finally saved enough money to buy his own a car. He was so proud of his new car. One night he was riding in this newly bought car and he stopped somewhere. A girl named Gloria jumped into his car. She sat right next to him and said, "let's go Jack". So, he drove, and he put his arm around her that she liked very much. He then put his hand down her blouse with her consent and he felt the biggest breasts he's ever touched.

Then, they got in the back seat had sex and it was the best sex he ever had among all the girls he had intimate relationships with. She wasn't bad looking, but he knew with her boldness she would never be a good girlfriend for him. If Jack got to first base with a girl the first time, he lost respect for her and in his mind that girl was a fallen woman.

Chiefly, he was more attracted to the girls that he had to work hard to get. He liked the girls that wouldn't let him get past her kneecap underneath all those crinolines. This was the kind of girl he wanted for a steady girlfriend. To his surprise they were hard to find.

For sure, he was always respectful of the girls he dated. He never advanced without their permission. If she said no, it was no, and he never pushed himself on any girl.

Although he was extremely popular with the girls, he still felt insecure being around girls. He had no enlightened awareness of how the girls perceived him. His low self-esteem and feelings of insecurity and feeling that he didn't fit in with others did not allow him to see that he was regarded by others with high esteem. His insecurities blocked him from seeing that the girls really liked him.

For this reason, he focused all his time on developing his basketball skills at the YMCA. Several very skilled teens from Albany, NY came to the Glen Falls YMCA, and he played basketball with them. Playing basketball with these talented skilled players from a different town helped him develop his basketball skills. Jack developed a competitive edge on all the players on his Glen Falls Junior Varsity and Varsity Basketball Team.

In fact, it was at the YMCA that he developed his famous deadly hook shot that caught the opposing team off guard all the time. He made his hook shots as easy as others breathe. He was an impact player and a star on his Junior Varsity and Varsity Basketball Team. Jack was an awesome athlete. He ran up and down the court making most every shot he took with ease. He was amazing to watch in action. He was a talented athlete that any coach would give their right arm to have on their team.

After each game the next day there was a write up in the local town newspapers referring to the varsity team as "**Rocco's Gems**", because the varsity basketball team was so awesome. They referred to Jack as the "Cape Canaveral Comet" listing all the hook shots and points he scored that night. They also referred to him as "**Pistol Jack**", because he was widely regarded as one of the greatest players on the team. Indeed, he was a spectacular showman.

On occasion his father would show up at the basketball game drunk and would yell unmercifully at the referee, coach, and Jack. This was so embarrassing for Jack. Some of the people in the stands would laugh at his father and others would cry because they knew how embarrassing his father's behavior was for him. His father had to be escorted out of the gym and was forbidden to come back in.

Interestingly, one night at a basketball game in high school Jack ran off the court uncontrollably and knocked down a girl. She was the most beautiful girl he ever laid eyes on. He asked her if she was OK and she replied "yes". Little did he know that evening that the woman he knocked down would be his future wife. Her name was Ann.

Moreover, he also played varsity baseball for four years in high school. He was their starting pitcher and was absolutely a star on the mound. He was so good that he got invited to try out for the Mets. When he arrived at the tryout session there were hundreds of kids trying out as well. Although he didn't get selected, he found it to be a great experience and was proud of himself for being invited.

In fact, he was recruited by the West Point coach to play baseball, but the guidance counselor did not advise Jack properly on application deadlines and specific requirements. This guidance counselor spoiled many students' opportunities to get into high powered colleges, because he never was on top of guiding the students.

To clarify, the counselor never knew about the required tests that had to be taken by students and the various application deadlines. Many of the students ended up applying late and therefore missed many golden opportunities. The counselor was long past his due retirement, wallowing around in the doom loop and could not care less whether students got into colleges or not. Unfortunately, Jack received no guidance on the requirements from his parents or the counselor and ended up applying too late to West Point.

Sadly, he grew up being mistrustful of people due to all the broken promises that he dealt with while growing up. He felt unloved. Once again, he thought if you can't trust your father who else can you trust. He couldn't understand what he did to deserve this awful treatment. He didn't realize it wasn't anything he did, it was his father's sociopathic and addictive behavior that was the problem and not anything he did.

Of course, this chaos manifested itself later as he exhibited patterns of insecure attachment, fear of potential rejection. He trusted so few people in his life. He had been burned by his father so many times it was hard for him to place trust in anyone. The only person as a child he trusted was Coach Rocco Polo.

For one thing, Jack had a love/hate relationship with his father. He hated him for all the abuse he perpetuated on him and his mother, but there was a part of his father that he loved too. He found it hard to understand. He saw him be very charismatic one minute and a raving maniac the next. This change in behavior at the drop of a hat confused him. He also sometimes saw his dad as a powerful man that impressed him.

In brief, one-time Jack got a ticket for the loud muffler on his car. Once again, this same policeman stopped him and gave him another ticket for the muffler. He told his father that this town policeman was on his back about the muffler again. Immediately, his father went to the policeman and threatened him. He told the policeman if he gave his son one more ticket there was going to be big trouble. That was the end of the tickets.

For this reason, there were times when Jack looked up to his father. The roller coaster of emotions he had and felt toward his father was extremely confusing and unsettling for Jack.

Markedly, while in school Jack displayed not only athletic talent but an artistic talent emerged. His art teacher was so impressed with a drawing he did of a modern-day train engine that she entered it in a local contest calling for drawings of trains, since Glen Falls was an old railroad town. Several other students' drawings were entered too. He won the contest and his drawing was displayed on the town sign saying, "Welcome to Glen Falls". Two of the best artists in the school were not happy that he won. His drawing was on that sign for years until recently. His drawing was taken down and another was put up. He never learned why his drawing was taken down.

Furthermore, a talent for singing emerged too. One day in music class his beautiful voice impressed the music teacher. He was asked to sing Silent Night solo at Midnight Mass one Christmas. After he sang, he received accolades from many people. Even his father was in church that night to hear him sing. Jack's mom said, "It's no wonder the church walls don't fall in with your father here tonight in church".

Interestingly, there was one event that stands out in Jack's mind while in high school. It was the time they had a Halloween party at the Glen Falls High School. He was sitting by himself in the bleachers and a girl dressed in a cat costume came up into the bleachers, leaned over to him and purred like a cat and then planted a big kiss on his cheek. She dashed away and he never knew who it was. For over 50 years he fanaticized who it may have been.

Since Jack was so handsome, was an extraordinary athlete, had a reputation for being respectful and just a nice guy he was incredibly attractive among the girls. Thus, he was quite popular in high school. He was voted among his classmates in the ninth grade to be their class president. There were two other very bright male classmates who were already preparing their resumes for college and were not too happy that Jack was voted the Class President. At graduation Jack was awarded the Most Valuable Player Award for his significant achievements as a baseball pitcher.

In between his school and athletic responsibilities, Jack worked as a caddy at the local country club. One of the men he caddied for a very prominent businessman from New York City. He was a short bald man who demanded respect. He had the most beautiful golf shoes that Jack ever saw and commented on them to the man. The man responded by saying "they better be nice; they are leather, and hand stitched in Italy. I have a pair in every color".

Surprisingly, one day a helicopter landed on the Green and the businessman said, "I have an emergency and have to go", and off he went up in the helicopter back to NYC. He made sure Jack got paid before he left. No one ever learned what the emergency was. The man always paid the caddies very well, but he had a demeanor of superiority about him.

Occasionally, the businessman hit a ball in the woods and never retrieved it. After Jack got paid at the end of the day, Jack went back to the exact spot where the ball was hit in the woods and picked it up. The balls were brand new and beautiful.

In fact, the prominent man specifically requested Jack as his caddy, because showing respect came naturally for Jack, having a father that demanded the same. He knew how to respond to authoritative figures at a young age, because Jack learned if he didn't cow tow to his father he'd be threatened to death. Having to cow tow to the businessman suited Jack simply fine, because he always paid him on time with a handsome tip.

In particular, the businessman was very vocal and was highlighted in the newspaper a lot and on TV as a member of the newly founded popular business organization. His competitors feared him, so they hired an ex con to shoot him at one of the businessmen's functions. Although he survived the attack, the businessman was almost completely paralyzed from the three bullet wounds. That ended his golfing days. He died seven years later of congestive heart failure related to his paralyzed condition. When Jack saw this on TV, it brought back vivid memories of his days when he caddied for this very prominent businessman.

Finally, as Jack grew older, he was able to stash a little money away without his father knowing about it and bought an inexpensive used car. After a while Jack wanted to upgrade his car and his father said "OK, I'll sell your car for you". He sold Jack's car and kept the money. His father did this same thing several times. Jack got some more money saved, bought a newer car, and his father sold it and again and kept the money.

For one thing, his father had no empathy for others. He used people to support his drunken addiction and had no feeling of remorse for what he did. Sadly, his father left his children hungry, his wife penniless, and the entire family were left with little essentials to barely get by. He could not care less about anyone but himself. He left a trail of destruction in everything he did, leaving his victims in lasting shock.

Repulsively, his father was manipulative and cunning and antagonized others. He could be very charming at times and had high intelligence and took advantage of those characteristics to use people for his benefit. He was totally unreliable and irresponsible. He had poor judgment and never learned by experience. He was untruthful and insincere and continually ignored the rights of others. He showed no regard to right and wrong. He treated others harshly and with callous indifference and didn't understand how his actions affected others.

Actually, he saw the consequences, but just didn't care. He lacked remorse, shame, or guilt for how he ignored his family responsibilities, and how he embarrassed his family in front of others, and how the chaos he created impacted on his children.

Additionally, he was incapable of loving others but was good at faking emotions of love in order to get what he wanted. Everything he did was self-serving for his own good. He was a master manipulator. He had no long-term friends because he'd drive them away, so he had a revolving door of friends. He had a lifelong syndrome of misbehavior, abuse, bullying, deceitfulness, uncaring and irresponsibility.

With this in mind, Jack's father met a physician somewhere and in conversation his father lied and told the physician he was a private detective. They talked several times after that, and the physician said I think I can use your services. He explained to Jack's father that he thought his wife was cheating, and he wanted to know who the other man was. He asked his father if he thought he could do that. Jack's father responded sure, but I'll need two thousand down and rest can be paid when he identified the man.

Explicitly, every week the physician asked for a report and of course he had nothing to report and kept saying "I'm working on it". His father had no camera, no binoculars or any of the tools a private investigator typically used to track down people of interest. His father did locate the wife, however, and as charming as he could be, he ended up having an affair with the physician's wife. After he had no reports for the physician, his father was fired, and the doctor was scammed for two thousand dollars.

All his father's behavior confused Jack immensely. Jack observed that his father was very likeable and endearing sometimes. One moment he was as charming as could be and people were attracted to him and in the next moment, he was a wild maniac. Jack could never figure out why and how he could change his personality at a moment's notice.

Indeed, this is what made it so scary for Jack because his father's behavior was so unpredictable. He never knew which father he was going to see, the charming one or the bully one. This created intense stress within all the children.

On a positive side, during high school he came to his friend Mary's house frequently. He fell madly in love with her cousin Pat. She lived in Falls Church, Virginia and he only saw her when she visited Mary. One summer she came up to Glen Falls, NY to visit Mary. Jack was so excited to learn that Pat was coming up to visit Mary. He was looking forward to seeing her.

Shockingly, when Pat came to visit, she told Jack when she graduated from high school, she was going into the convent to become a nun. He was devastated when she broke the news to him. He really loved her and knew the news ended their future together.

Also, he met another girl named Megan at Mary's house who he had a crush on too. She lived in the Bronx and only came up during the summer and stayed somewhere near Rick Banks's farm. He found a way to visit her in the Bronx and got the feeling her parents were not crazy about him. She was extremely bright and attended a very prestigious Science High School in the Bronx. It was exceedingly difficult to gain admission to that school. He felt that she was totally out of his league and over time did not see her anymore.

Frequently, he spent his free time at Mary's house with her friends. Mary had a juke box in her parent's house located in the finished basement. It had a pool table too and was a favorite hangout for Mary's friends. Mary taught Jack how to dance and he invited her to his first prom because he felt comfortable with her.

During the prom, a girl named Tina kept interrupting Mary and Jack so she could dance with him. Jack and Mary doubled dated with Tina Banks and Mike Capehart. Tina had a mad crush on Jack Long and after the prom she switched the seating arrangements. She sat in the back with him forcing Mary to sit up front with Mike. This annoyed the daylights out of Jack. He thought Mary didn't want to be with him and Mary thought Jack didn't want to be with her, and God only knows what Mike thought. Of interest it wasn't until 50 years later Jack learned it wasn't Mary that made the switch, it was Tina.

## Post High School Days

When he graduated from high school, Jack's father wanted him to get a job as a door to door fuller brush salesman. After the first door closed in his face, he said I'm not doing this. He wanted to go to college. He went to a local Community College but had to withdraw due to lack of finances. He couldn't pay the tuition or buy gas for the car. Of course, his father was not there to lend support for him to go to college.

Actually, he resorted to stealing gas from other cars, so he could drive to college. This was totally out of character for Jack, but he was desperate and wanted to go to college so badly. He occasionally would hitch a ride with a friend Janice Swihart, the girl he had a crush on in elementary school. But he could not depend on that, because their class schedules were different. He became worried that he'd get caught stealing gas and have to deal with his father, so he stopped that behavior of stealing gas and got a job at a chemical company as a mechanic.

In time, Jack started dating a girl he really liked named Nancy Nelson. But the relationship broke off. He was sitting on the steps of a building looking sad and dejected. Ann Marlowe, the girl he ran off the court when playing basketball in high school, came along and said "Jack, what's wrong--you look so sad". She sat on the steps with him and he proceeded to tell her about the breakup. He was impressed with her empathy for him. She had a crush on him stemming back to high school. He went on to date another girl and although Ann still had a crush on him, she had a boyfriend at this time.

As fate would have it later, he ran into Ann at a local diner. Ann had just come from her cousin's wedding and was dressed in a gorgeous gown. She saw Jack by his car that had broken down in the parking lot. She went over to him to say hello. She still had a mad crush on him. He looked up a couldn't take his eyes off her she was so beautiful. He asked her for her number. A few days later they started dating.

After one of the dates he brought her home and he gave her a goodbye kiss and she put her leg up like you see in the movies. She lost her balance and the two of them fell off the four-foot porch that had no railing. He fell on top of her and her mother came out and said what are you doing to my daughter? They both explained and in the house she went.

At this time, when he was dating Ann steadily, his father met her parents one evening. On the first meeting his father said to her parents "Jack is nothing but a bum, he has no job", implying he was a loser and would never make anything of himself as he was in between jobs. Jack was mortified that his father would say something as mean as that his front of his girlfriend's parents. He was hurt, embarrassed and those words weighed heavy on his heart. His father was a total demoniac monster.

Jack while dating never had any money or a car to take Ann out. He hitchhiked to her house; and many of their dates were just spending time together high on love. Occasionally, they would double date with a couple who had a car and they went out for pizza. Jack had to save money all month for these occasions so he could pay for his portion of the pizza. This kind of a date was a huge deal to Jack.

One night he was hitchhiking home and he got into a car with several rough characters in the back seat that he didn't see until he got in the car. He was terrified thinking they were going to kill him. The driver said don't be scared we wont harm you. A bit relieved, but still terrified. He told the driver to drop him off at an intersection that was five miles from his house. When he got out, he was so happy to be alive.

In due time, he and Ann fell deeply in love with each other and became engaged after dating for one year. In fact, it was Ann who proposed to Jack. Jack said yes and they went out to buy the ring. They enjoyed each other's company and had so much fun together.

By this time, he finally had a car and they went out to a popular place where young folks hung out. Jack and Ann ran into one of her former boyfriends who was being menacing with Ann. Jack told him to buzz off that they were engaged. The ex-boyfriend was still in love with Ann and would not accept the fact that she was now engaged to someone else. The ex-boyfriend came up to Ann and said "you're not engaged to him". And she said "yes, I am", and he called Ann a liar. Jack got upset. The ex-boyfriend had several friends with him, and they were going to beat Jack up. The owner of the establishment asked Jack to leave and he replied by saying why me, he 's the one causing trouble?

It just so happened, that another guy watching this whole scene came over to Jack and he said don't worry I have several friends here, more than they have, and I'll watch your back. So, Ann and Jack left the establishment. The guy he never met protected them as they left the place. Jack was incredibly grateful to him for looking after them and safe guarding their exit.

With attention to another night, Jack and his fiancé Ann and others were members of bowling league. They were bowling one evening and the team was one person down. The members asked Jack's father who was there also to fill in. He refused and went to the bar to have a drink. So, the league team had to bowl with a handicap of one down.

After the bowling was over that evening, Jack and his fiancé Ann went out to the car to go home. His father came running out like a lunatic yelling give me that engagement ring I want to see if Jack overpaid for the ring. He tried to get it off Ann's finger and she refused to give it to him. It was so embarrassing for Jack and terrifying for Ann. He probably was going to give the ring to the bartender to get more drinks.

While engaged Ann had a guy at her workplace that was constantly hitting up on her and refused to accept the fact that she was engaged, He constantly tried to talk her out of the engagement and told her she didn't' really love Jack.

The other ex-boyfriend continued to try to see Ann also even though they were engaged. The entire time Ann and Jack were engaged they had to put up with these two guys that were madly in love with Ann, who refused to accept that she was engaged. These two guys made their lives miserable.

Surely, Ann captured Jack's heart and after eight months of being engaged, they were married at St. Francis Church, Glen Falls, New York. They got married November 23,1963, the day after Kennedy was shot. He was 20 years old and Ann was 19 years old. They both saved all year to pay for their wedding. They had a magnificent joyful, fun filled, beautiful wedding. The ring bearer was Jacks younger brother who was five and he walked down the aisle and when he saw his Mom, he went in the pew with her and he had to be prodded to go to the altar. The junior bridesmaid was the same age and she was pulling the beads off Ann's gown and was eating them during the wedding ceremony.

At the reception everyone had a wonderful time. When Ann and Jack cut the cake, she shoved the piece of cake in his face. And then when it was his turn to cut the cake, he chased her around the table and stuffed the cake in her face. All done in fun and laughter, The guests all loved this part of the wedding reception.

They spent their honeymoon in the Birchwood Poconos. This was the highlight of his life, living with Ann. Married to a woman who idolized him and who he loved dearly.

When they left for their honeymoon. Jack gave his father fifty dollars to pay for his car insurance while he was gone. His father spent the money and never paid the car insurance bill. When he and Ann came back from their honeymoon the insurance company almost cancelled their insurance due to late payment.

Always scrounging around for booze money his father cashed checks that bounced due to insufficient funds to cover them. He did this several times and caused a major problem with the bank. The bank eventually refused to honor any checks written by his father and this was an embarrassment for his wife. The bank no longer would do business with his mom or father.

Par for the course another night his father came home in the middle of the night and beat the pulp out of his mom. Jack was married now and was not living at home. The next day Jack came to visit his mom and saw bruises all over her body. She complained of headaches. He freaked and immediately took his mom to the hospital. When she returned home, she told him to take the rifle to his apartment because she knew her husband was going to kill her. He complied and took the rifle to his apartment.

Shortly after that episode his father came home at 3AM one morning and asked his younger brother where his mom was. His brother replied he didn't know. So, the father went to Jack's apartment and was banging on the doors and windows, ranting and raving, wakening all the neighbors. The apartment literally shook with the pounding on the door and windows. Jack's wife and sister in the apartment at the time were terrified and hid in a closet. Jack got the rifle and said about his father, "If he finds a way to get in here, I will shoot him with the rifle". Jack held the rifle, shaking in fear with beads of sweat pouring off his forehead. Finally, his father left, and Jack felt ill thinking how close he came to shooting his own father with the rifle.

At this point, Jack had occasional feelings wishing his father would die. Jack and his father had a verbal altercation and shortly after that argument Jack's father gave him a coat for his birthday. Jack gave the coat back to his mother and said, "Tell my father to shove this coat up his ass".

At the time when his father passed on Jack suffered with an overwhelming sense of guilt. He played that verbal altercation and the non-acceptance of his father's gift over and over in his mind, tormenting himself. Even when his father passed, he continued to torture Jack from the grave.

Sadly, after his father died his mom began to drink heavily and had different men swing by the house and Jack suspected she was having relations with them. One night he came home to check on his mom and found a man in the house and he chased him out.

Despite this behavior of his mom, he loved her dearly. He protected her his entire life. And he would do anything humanly possible for his mom. He knew she loved him, and he'd do anything for his beloved mother.

For sure, Jack appreciated all the practical living skills his mother taught him. For example, the sewing lessons came in particularly handy later in life. He learned how to sew patches on his athletic bags to identify that they belonged to him. Also, one time he went to a wedding at West Point, New York with a pair of pants that were tailor made especially for Jack. As he walked in the Thayer Hotel his wife said, "I hate to tell you this, but your ass is wide open". He reached back and lo and behold the seamstress forgot to sew the crotch up. He went to the front desk of the hotel and begged for a needle and thread. It took a while for the desk clerk to find a needle and thread.

Finally, they found what he needed, and he went into the men's room and sewed up the crotch himself. Thank God, he thought, for the sewing lesson from his mom.

In short, during Jack's entire childhood his father modeled drinking, he was a role model for abusive behavior and bullying. He saw firsthand his father's display of irresponsibility, untrustworthiness, and cunning behavior. He witnessed the degrading of his mom as his father called her names and threatened physical, violence.

His father modeled criminal behavior by driving while drunk, cashing bad checks, stealing money, and assaulting people. Jack observed him create emotional chaos by yelling at the family members, neighbors, coaches, and referees. He role modeled infidelity by chasing every woman in town.

For this reason, and with the unpredictability of his father's behavior he could never bring any of his friends' home. He never knew what to expect when he walked into the house. It was so sad for him to see other friends with warm loving fathers. He longed to know what that felt like to have a loving father and a calm household.

Sadly, his mom suffered from severe physical, psychological, and verbal abuse on an ongoing basis. She was a victim of abusive behavior, threats, and assaults. Thus, he grew up with no parents. His parents both let him down. Even though his mom did not have the psychic energy, courage or financial resources or community resources to remove Jack and other siblings from this horrific environment he still loved her dearly.

Whenever he got in to trouble with his father, she came to his rescue, saying she did whatever his father was upset with. She didn't want him to get a beating and protected him whenever she could. He always knew his mom loved him. Although she was limited in her ability to help the children, he always felt that she was the glue that held him together.

Inasmuch as, he felt respect, love and dignity from his mother Jack never felt he belonged to family and this feeling was a dangerous hurt, because it had the power to break his heart, his spirit and sense of self-worth. To repeat, when you feel your father doesn't love you, who else could he feel he belonged to or be loved by.

Important to realize, there were constant, no-holds barred battles between his father and mother that made him feel shame and he lived with the secrecy of shame. He felt alone, unworthy of love and unworthy of belonging. He felt he was the only one among his classmates living through this "shit show".

Thus, he began to believe the words "hope and faith" were just that words. He doubted the existence of God. Because if there was a God why would he expose his mother, his siblings and him to the horrific abuse they all experienced. He began to believe that everything that was happening was his fault and he felt helpless to cure it. His soul became cold. He lived in constant pain and found his primary outlet for not belonging in focusing on sports.

To Jack's credit unlike his brother he did not relieve his pain by inflicting pain on others. If it were not for Coach Rocco, he would have passed the pain on to his siblings and son. He learned how to find the courage to own his own pain and develop empathy and compassion for others in a unique way.

On a positive side, Coach Rocco taught him how to lose with dignity, how to be a team player, how to respect others. He learned what hard work meant and what it took to persevere through difficulties. Jack learned the meaning of commitment and the importance of maintaining a never give up attitude. He took the lessons taught by Coach Polo to heart and appreciated the time and interest Coach Polo took in him.

Markedly, Coach Rocco was aware that that Jack was being raised in a dysfunctional family, but was never aware of the extent of the abuse that took place. It was a big family dark secret and everyone in the family pretended all was just fine. Coach Rocco tucked him under his wing, always guiding him in the right direction. Jack felt like Coach was his second father. The one he always dreamed of having.

Once again, back in the era when this story started, they did not have the support for battered women that exists now. His mom had no financial ability to remove the children from the intense toxic environment. She knew if she left him, he would kill her. She did the best she could with the minimal resources she had.

Surely, after reading the childhood of Jack, one may question why he didn't tell a teacher, priest, or a school counselor about the abuse. As a reminder Jack was raised in the 50's and teacher, counselors and even priests were not trained how to handle problems like this in those days. And Jack would never do it anyway because of overwhelming fear of what his father would do if he found out that he told someone.

One may also wonder why Jack didn't stand up more to his father when he abused his mother. The fact is he did whenever he was at home. Each time his father physically threatened or actually abused his mom and whenever his father took out his aggressions on his mom like a rag doll in his presence, he got right in front of his mom, staring his father in is hung over glazed face. He looked right at his violent angry bulging eyes and told his father if he hurts his mom, he will have to hurt him first. He always took the risk of protecting his mom. He loved his mom more than life itself.

The emotional chains of fear of harm, lack of trust, anger, fear of abandonment, emotional confusion, fear of authority, emotional chaos, anxiety, guilt, social isolation, and feeling a need to be perfect shackled our friend. These emotional chains had a major impact on his ability to feel joy, to feel comfortable in social situations and to experience happiness. He had no peace in his heart. His childhood was a total nightmare filled with gruesome, atrocious, physical abuse that no child should ever experience.

# 2

# BREAKING THE CYCLE OF ABUSE

**THANK GOD JACK** had a surrogate parent in his basketball Coach Rocco Polo in high school. Coach Polo developed Jack' self-efficacy and made him believe his effort and hard work mattered. He instilled a belief that he was able to achieve his goals and complete his tasks. Coach described his unique gifts and how he overcame significant struggles during the game that made him feel he could accomplish anything. He made him feel he was an impact player on the court. He made him believe in himself and let him know his contributions were significant and mattered.

In fact, Jack felt nothing could stop him. He developed a sense of relevance inside himself. He knew exactly what his role was and how hard work contributed to the team. Coach showed him how he measured his progress so he could set goals to improve. He felt valued, relevant, and powerful. Coach created an environment of encouragement that had a huge impact on his personal life, his future goals and how he perceived himself. His encouragement carried over into his private life by instilling the values of hard work, compassion, cooperation, loyalty, and enthusiasm leading his life toward personal growth and success.

Indeed, they had a special relationship that influenced Jack by encouraging him toward excellence in all aspects of his life. He built trust which made the relationship authentic thus opening effective lines of communication. All of Coach Polo's efforts payed off big time for Jack.

Above all, Jack refused to give in to the victim mentality, found his strengths, capitalized on them, and took responsibility and broke the horrific cycle of abuse as he grew older. He was determined that he was not going to be like his father in any way. He was not going to give in to alcoholism, womanize or abuse and bully others. He rejected all the put downs and labels that his father placed on him and clung to the values he learned from Coach Polo.

For one thing, to make sure this addiction was not passed on to his family, he raised up to put a stop to it and broke the generational curse and passed down the generational blessing. He was able to leave his dark past behind and let go of the past.

At this time, he and Ann were now married, madly in love with each other and they had a mutual respect. She was a virgin when he married her. And as badly as he wanted her while they were engaged, he held off his impulses and fierce desires and waited till the day they got married. This was the kind of girl he always dreamed of marrying. On their honeymoon they finally had sexual intercourse. He went gentle with her did not push her in any way. For Ann it was painful and probably not the ecstasy she expected the first time. Over time she became more accustomed to the act, and in time enjoyed intimacy and had an incredibly happy, successful romantic relationship with Jack.

For sure, she loved him profoundly and never over all the years of their marriage refused to engage in sex when Jack made advances. She never once came up with I'm too tired, I have a headache, I don't feel well. They had a marriage made in heaven. To this day he has never fallen prey for other women's propositions. He's been faithful and never once had an affair. Jack took his vows extremely seriously and loved his wife more than life itself. He had Ann on a pedestal and admired every wonderful quality she possessed.

After three years of marriage in 1966 Jack, Jr. was born; he was the largest baby in the hospital at 8 pounds 12 ounces They were overjoyed with the birth of their newborn son. Both Ann and Jack were determined to provide Jack, Jr. with every possible opportunity to be successful. They were both willing and determined to put their needs on the back burner to raise Jack to grow up not only self-sufficient, and successful, but grow up to be a nice person.

Explicitly, Jack knew in order to achieve this goal he had to break the cycle of abuse. He had to guard the doorway to his mind and refused to let his father's labels take a stronghold on his thinking and only let the values of his coach to enter his mind. He nourished the values handed down to him by Coach Polo, embraced and operationalized them which allowed Jack to rise above the storm of his past like an eagle. Jack was successful in moving on and eventually become the warmest, most loving father to his son and a faithful, committed husband that any woman would give their right arm to have. He felt blessed. He believed the challenges of the past had made him strong inside.

By all means, he chose to rise up and said with God's help I'm turning the tide. He set a new standard. He was not going to be an alcoholic, he was not going to be a womanizer, he was not going to be disrespectful of others. He was not going to pattern his behavior after his father's. He changed his thinking and refused to be a victim anymore. He enlarged his vison and chose to be a champion in life.

Significantly, his whole life was devoted to instilling the values that would lead him to a successful life. He wanted to show his son what it was like to be loved, respected, and trusted and to live life with integrity. He wanted his son Jack, Jr. to grow up feeling self-assured, self-confident, warm, loving, and giving. And Jack achieved that goal. His son grew up with all the values, qualities and virtues and turned out to be a wonderful person who loves his parents dearly.

Truly, Jack over his entire life continued to delete all the negative labels his father put in his mind. Namely, that Jack would never amount to much, that he was not talented, that he was not smart, that he was a loser. He wiped out all the feelings of inferiority, anxiety, intimidation, fear, unworthiness and guilt out of his mind. He reprogrammed his thoughts and filled his mind with the positive labels that his coach put on him. Coach Polo put labels on Jack that communicated you are bright, talented, strong, athletic, hardworking, victorious and respectful. You're a valued impact team player. As Jack filled his mind with Coach Polo's labels that were placed on Jack, the chains loosened, and the cycle of abuse was broken. He woke up his dreams, talents and potential and set a new standard. He broke the barrier and realized he was filled with greatness and turned his thinking around with better thoughts.

To point out, Jack, Sr. was extremely intelligent, had insight and was inspired to break the cycle of abuse. His main goal in life was to be a role model father by becoming the warmest loving father he knew how to become, and role model husband. He achieved these two goals in a stellar manner.

In fact, to this day Coach Polo had no idea what an impact he had on developing Jack's character. Jack was truly fortunate to have Coach Rocco Polo serve as mentor and a surrogate father to Jack. Coach Polo mentored him and tucked Jack under his arm, always directing him in the right direction with Jack's best interest at heart. Jack looked up to and admired Coach Polo. One can only speculate how Jack would have turned out if he did not have Coach Polo take an interest in him.

Surprisingly, Jack who is now 77 and Coach Rocco is 93 and they still keep in touch by phone and make occasional visits to see each other. They talk about the Rocco Gems, politics, and sports. They live in the same town making the face to face visits easy on both. Coach Rocco owns a home on the Jersey shore and offered it to Jack and Ann to stay for a couple of weeks. They took him up on his offer and had a wonderful time. The only instructions Coach Rocco left was" leave the place the way you found it".

With attention to Jack and Ann they loved traveling to different parts of the US and abroad. One trip that stands out in Jack's mind is their trip to Hershey Park in Pennsylvania. They were on a tour of the candy factory. Their son crossed the yellow line barrier and went right up the woman making the candy kisses and she gave him a handful of candy kisses. He was so excited his smile went from ear to ear and showed his mom and dad the candies he received with such joy and pride. The tour guide took Jack aside and scolded Jack for letting his son cross the barrier.

Of course, Jack didn't have the heart to chastise his son because he was so excited, and he said to himself well that's what life's all about-- you grab as much as you can get and the tour guide let it go. Shortly after that incident the factory tours were discontinued.

Specifically, one of Ann's favorite places to visit was Virginia Beach. Their son was a teenager then and he wanted to scope out the boardwalk by himself. A normal teenager asserting his autonomy and independence. But after a while Ann and Jack became concerned where he was. So, they went walking the entire boardwalk and finally saw him coming out a game arcade with a guy his age that looked like the incredible hulk. His son said, "Meet my new friend". Jack asked his son to step aside so he could speak to him in private, and Jack said, "Son are you going to be OK". His son replied, "Oh sure- who is going to mess with us when I'm with muscle man". Jack has always trusted his son's judgment and so he let him continue to explore the boardwalk, but they kept a close eye on him without being intrusive.

While on the boardwalk the next day Jack noticed that the hot dog vendor wasn't doing much business. Jack said get a couple of girls in bikinis to go out on the beach and take the orders and you'll increase your business. And that's exactly what the vendor did. The business picked up so dramatically that he couldn't keep up with all the hot dog orders. Jack passed the hot dog owner the following day and said, "See, I told you that strategy would work". The man didn't even offer Jack a free hot dog for his advice.

Later that day Jack saw a homely man on the beach with a black snake. As the young girls in bikinis walked by, he'd invite them to pet his snake. It was disgusting. He was hoping that one of the girls would pet his other snake. Jack said he heard of men using dogs as a catalyst to meet girls, but a snake he's never heard of before.

While visiting Virginia Beach they met a couple from Rochester, New York who knew their son when he was working in a sports bar as a waiter. His son waited on this couple. They had a five-year-old daughter who loved dolphins. Jack and Ann bought her a stuffed dolphin that she fell in love with it. Together they all went on a dolphin watch boat. The little girl sat up front in the boat and after a long time there were no sightings of any dolphins. So, she leaned over the rail of the boat and said, "Come here, Baby" and suddenly, the dolphins appeared, and they stuck their heads up to look at her. It was so adorable.

Also, while in Virginia Beach Ann and Jack enjoyed watching the fishing boats coming in and loved watching the men clean 200-pound tuna. A sight rarely seen. Everything about Virginia Beach was exciting and fun for both Ann and Jack.

Another beach site they loved was Daytona Beach. When they arrived, it rained for four solid days. Jack and Ann got to know a couple Jim and Donna in the next hotel room who had two children. They were from Toronto, Canada. The children came in their room and played with Jack's son's toys and had a ball. The two couples became friends over the years.

While there at Daytona they watched the speed boats that go over 200 miles an hour. An exciting sight to say the least. They took the children to a penned in fishing pond and with bamboo poles using shrimp as bait, they brought in a lot of fish. They went back to the hotel and had a giant fish fry. Jack cleaned all the fish they caught.

Excitingly, the two couples decided to take the children to Disney World. Jim was a professional sailor and went on Space Mountain. When he got off, he said he'd rather fight a war than go on Space Mountain again. The next day they went back to the Disney park and now Jack's son wanted to go on Space Mountain. So, they headed right over to the ride. Jack sat behind Ann and his son and he swears they still have his fingerprints ingrained in the bar he was holding on to so tightly. Ann thought Jack halfway through the ride had a heart attack.

Indeed, Jack and Ann lived a rich filled life and had so much fun together. They went on over 30 cruises, eating and drinking like a king and queen. They were a magnetic power couple that people gravitated to and wanted to sit with them at dinner on the cruises. The captains of the ships always invited them to sit at their table for dinner. They enjoyed so much stopping at the various ports to eat, shop and see all the new sights.

In fact, it didn't matter where they went, they just loved being with one another, whether it was at home together playing cards, going to concerts, horse track racing in upstate New York, sunbathing on the beach or dining on a cruise. Life was good!

Namely, Jack, Sr. gave his son a good name and modeled what a truehearted devoted husband was and what a doting, caring father was. Jack's primary goal in life was to show his son what it meant to be loved, respected, trusted and to live life with strong moral principles. His whole life as he raised Jack, Jr. was devoted to instilling the values that would lead his son to a successful life filled with self-fulfillment. They provided Jack Jr. many rich opportunities and experiences. Jack made sure his son graduated from college debt free. As a result, not only is their son successful career wise, but he grew up being a kind, compassionate, generous person. Jack Jr is generous to his parents, co-workers, and friends. He walks along the streets in San Diego giving money, clothes, and hugs to the homeless. In fact, he actually gave a homeless man with no shoes his clogs to wear as he walked home barefoot. He possesses an upbeat, positive outgoing attitude. He is well liked by many and held in high esteem by those who know him.

Surely, they were so proud of their son and enjoyed every minute of raising him. He was a good kid when growing up. Jack and Ann never had a bit of trouble with him in any way. He was extraordinarily successful as an adult, and this made their hearts glow. Nothing pleases Ann and Jack more than when their son visits or calls. He is the joy of their life. Both Ann and Jack feel that giving birth to Jack, Jr. was the greatest achievement in their life.

Likewise, Jack, Jr. loves his parents and appreciates all the sacrifices they made for him. He is always there in time of need as his parents grew older. Jack and Ann did a spectacular job raising their son. Jack, Jr. possessed all the wonderful qualities any parent would be proud of.

## Working Years

Ann and Jack both loved their careers. Jack worked at a Chemical Plant that made a broad array of industrial chemicals, synthetic fibers, petroleum-based fuels, lubricants, building materials, and agricultural chemicals. Jack worked in the mechanical engineering department and serviced the tanks that held the materials and the trucks that transported the materials. He was a brilliant talented mechanic.

To emphasize, as an adult Jack's past feelings of helplessness led to an intense need for perfection. He became overly rigid at his workplace. He was bound and determined to learn every aspect of his job with perfection. He took advantage of every older wise mentors on the job and became a stellar student and valued employee. Jack tried to learn everything he possibly could. Other employees disregarded older, wiser men, but not Jack.

Over time, he knew more about the equipment, tanks, trucks, and engines than anyone on the job. Jack became seen as a valued employee who was knowledgeable, dependable and an expert at what he did. If anyone had a major problem, they immediately called Jack, and he always knew how to fix the major problems. He made sure he had a key that opened every door, truck, storeroom in case he was called in the middle of the night to fix a problem, which occurred frequently. His key ring must have weighed 10 pounds with all the keys on the chain ring. He frequently got called in the middle of the night to fix some major problem that arose.

Surprisingly, Jack had perfect attendance every year. He only missed two days all the years of employment, namely, a major toothache and a day of vomiting incessantly. He was at work every day at 4 AM. He arrived before anyone else in the plant did.

Specific problems arose on the job every day. One night there was a leak in a huge tank that contained glue. Some ignoramus said I'll fix it. He got a ladder and climbed up to where the leak was, and he put his hand over it to stop it. Glue started leaking down his hand, his arm and down his leg and he was stuck on the tank and started yelling at the top of his lungs for help. Several employees had to go up and peel him off the tank. Jack went up with the proper tools and equipment and fixed the leak.

Moreover, another time a truck was going down the interstate and blue glue was leaking out of the truck onto the highway. The State Police stopped the truck and the truck driver called Jack for help. Jack arrived on the scene and found that an employee didn't lock a device, and that's what caused the leak. Jack fixed the lock mechanism and then poured a substance on the highway all the way back to where the leak started many miles away. The substance Jack cleverly poured on the highway blended in with pavement, so the blue glue was disguised.

Truly, there are countless examples of major problems that popped up that Jack was called into to fix, because he was the only one who knew how to assess, diagnose, and fix the problem. Some problems were in the plant and some were on the road.

During Jack's career he witnessed some serious accidents. He even came close to being killed on the job himself. When he first started his career at Dupont Jack was helping a carpenter perform a job and they had to wear safety glasses that were approved for eye wear. While the carpenter was pounding screw nails, Jack took off his glasses for just a second and put them back on when the carpenter hit the nail and it went flying and put a hole in Jack's glasses. He went to the manager and said what the hell kind of glasses are these look at this hole in the glasses, and the manager said you're damn lucky to be alive. They saved your life cause that screw had the power of a 22-rifle bullet and would have been driven right into your brain. Jack felt bad and lucky at the same time and from that day forward became very safety conscious. He actually got a pin to recognize him for saving his eyesight with the safety glasses.

Notably, there was another time that Jack got a piece hot metal in his eye. It was excruciatingly painful. He went to the supervisor. The supervisor took a towel and pulled it out and Jack felt immediate relief. It went into the white of the eye and not into the eye itself. Once again, he was extremely fortunate. He witnessed several other people not so fortunate who lost fingers, hands and other parts of the arm and were severely injured.

With attention to Jack's job it is important to mention that with his handsome looks and respect that he held within the company; this combo led to unrelenting propositions from the woman in the plant. He resisted all propositions, because he had an extraordinarily strong, loving, committed relationship with his wife Ann. This made him a well-respected employee. He was affectionately nicked name Sweet Jack by the women he worked with.

Unfortunately, his boss gave in to the propositions. His boss went out on his lunch hour and had a quick affair with a different woman each time. Word spread through the plant and his boss lost all respect from his employees. Word got back to his wife and it destroyed his third marriage. It was a nightmare for the men who got involved in an intimate manner.

Truly, Jack was a man of character. He saw what womanizing did to his family, when his father ran after every vulnerable woman in town. And he saw what it did to men in the workplace. It literally destroyed their marriages and their respect in the workplace. He had the insight, strength, and strong character to avoid such behavior no matter how tempting it may have been.

Once again, he attributes Rocco Polo his varsity Basketball Coach for developing his character so he could handle ethical, moral, career, and other challenges that arose in his life. Jack never fell to any of these temptations and was faithful to this day to his wife and never had an encounter with another woman during the 56 years of his marriage.

To point out, there was only one person at his place of work that did not like Jack. It was a man who was jealous of Jack's advancement within the corporation. He was a psychopath with absolutely no conscience. He made up stories about Jack, lied to Jack's boss and told his boss that Jack was doing things that were fabricated to put Jack in poor light with his boss. He started awful rumors among the employees.

Specifically, this psychopath tried to destroy Jack's life. Most compelling however for Jack was that his boss and subordinate employees knew Jack well enough to know the man was lying. But this man was relentless in his character assassinations of Jack. Thank God, over time this man was let go for buzzing around like a little mosquito generating negativities everywhere he went. Jack was finally free of his target. He enjoyed many years more of work. Finally, when Jack retired from the chemical plant as a mechanic, he received his gold watch and was incredibly grateful.

After he retired to his surprise, he missed work and the interaction it provided a great deal. So, he accepted a position at a company that was in the paper supply business. He was put in charge of a department that supervised many employees. He was seen as an exemplary leader and once again was a well-respected department head. He absolutely loved his boss Mike. His boss valued Jack's expertise and hard work.

Interestingly, Jack's boss coordinated several golf tournaments that were used as fund raisers for the Franciscan Friars. The boss always invited Jack to play in the tournament on his team. He recognized his athletic ability and stellar ability to play golf. They entered at least thirty tournaments over the years of work and always came in first or second. Each tournament ended with a grand celebration with a huge dinner and recognition ceremony. Because they came in first and second all the time, they were honored by sitting at the table with the

Friars. Of course, they had to behave themselves and had to avoid their dicey language.

In recognition of their fine placement in the golf tournament Jack got a dozen set of golf balls, a tournament pin and a plaque designating their final placement in the tournament. Jack and the boss always looked forward to these tournaments. As they both retired, they kept in touch and became good friends. They enjoyed talking about the old days at work and the fun they had participating in the multiple fundraising tournaments.

Notably Jack work many hours of overtime. With the exception of the tournaments he put his recreation needs of hunting, fishing, and weekly golf on the back burner. At this time, his whole life revolved around work. He saved all that money to provide a nice retirement nest egg for he and Ann for when they both retired for good.

With attention to Ann she was educated as an accountant, was good at what she did, but didn't like it. She took a position as a teacher's aide and worked with special needs children. She found her purpose. She loved the children and they loved her. She had a special knack of bonding with the children that no one else could achieve. Ann relayed a story to Jack that he got a kick out of. Apparently, one special needs student said, "Ann I love you more than a septic tank". The teachers said to her "What did he say"? She told them that his comment was the greatest gift she could have ever received because his father owned a septic tank company.

To be sure Jack grew to love the special needs children too. Ann was a very generous person. She donated many of her sick days to other colleagues who ran out of their sick leave before they recuperated from illness or surgery. She was always going the extra mile to help people in need. She thought about others before herself. Her grandmother always said to her "Ann you'd give away your asshole and shit out your ribs", meaning you are too generous to your own detriment. And generous she was.

Markedly, she looked after her husband and was always concerned about him. Always wanting to do whatever she could to lighten his load at work. She made him the best nutritious meals, did all the chores around the house including laundry, shopping, cleaning, all out of love for Jack. She never complained about her workload. She worshipped the ground he walked on, and Jack placed Ann on a pedestal. It was a marriage made in heaven. They loved being together, going places together and doing kind things for each other.

Sadly, the only thing missing in his life at this point was a warm loving relationship with his younger brother. Jack was upset with his brother Jimmy because he treated his mom poorly in Jack's eyes. His brother verbally abused her when he was a kid. And as an adult Jimmy would park his car in front of his mom's house and then went jogging. Never once did he have the common courtesy to go in and visit his mom to see if she needed anything.

And one-time Jack's son from Albany High School played against Jimmy's high school where he was a coach. Jack's son's team won, and Jimmy never congratulated his son. He just disconfirmed his son and made an angry comment: "Well what do you expect, you have all those minority basketball players on your team, of course you're going to win," totally downplaying Jack's son's abilities and achievements in the game. Jack's son and Jack's feelings were hurt. Jack always felt Jimmy looked down on Jack because he didn't have a college degree like Jimmy.

Important to realize when Jack's mom died Jimmy went to her house and threw out many of her possessions in the garbage, even presents that Jack gave to her over the years. His brother kept the valuable items including all the family pictures and never shared any of them with Jack. He never out of courtesy ask Jack to come over to help sort through the items and to provide him with an opportunity to take some of the sentimental items he may have wanted. Jimmy never shared any of the family pictures with Jack, that was so hurtful to him personally.

Chiefly, Jimmy as an adult developed a severe character disorder where he had an inflated sense of his own importance and had a deep need for excessive attention and admiration. He lacked empathy for others and had difficulty establishing effective relationships with people. He was preoccupied with fantasies of unlimited success, brilliance, and power. He was selfish, arrogant, demanding, and exploited others. This narcissism was like a balloon that needed admiration, attention, and compliments on how wonderful he was to keep the balloon inflated. When the attention and admiration was lacking the balloon started to deflate, then he resorted to arousing negative emotions to undermine people's self-esteem and to keep them off balance and insecure. This made him feel superior to others.

Namely, he did this with Jack and his wife as he called them losers, and trash. He was projecting how he saw himself onto his brother Jack. The negative unwarranted labels, criticism and blame he placed on Jack and his family was a way to cover up his low self-esteem and shame he had all brought on by his abusive father. He modeled exactly how his father behaved. The only way he could feel good about himself when his balloon was deflated was to put Jack down.

Moreover, he responded to Jack with heated arguments, criticism, and ridicule. He told Jack he was jealous of him, when in fact Jimmy was jealous of Jack. Jack was always popular as a kid in high school unlike Jimmy. Jack had a beautiful devoted wife and a great kid. Jack seemed so happy and Jimmy was not, so he lashed out negative comments to try and hurt his brother and family. Jack always got a double dose of verbal abuse, because he was the spitting image of his father. He was like a carbon copy of his father in looks. Every time his brother saw Jack all he could see was his father and projected a large dose of verbal abuse on Jack and his family.

Seemingly so, Jimmy was not able to rise above the abusive, controlling experience of his father like Jack. He led and continues to lead a very unhappy life. Jimmy exploited his younger brother Paul by convincing him that Jack was jealous of him and that Jack and his family were losers. It gave him a sense of power to be able to brainwash and control his younger brother. He talked his younger brother into writing a letter to Jack outlining criticisms that Jimmy put in his head.

Jimmy was one sick cookie.

A point of fact is that his younger brother was five years old when Jack got married and twelve years old when his dad died. So, the youngest brother did not experience the amount of abuse that the two older brothers experienced. He spent more time with Jimmy then Jack, because Jack was out of the household as his younger brother Paul grew up.

Notably, Jack and his wife bent over backwards into a pretzel trying to develop a relationship with Jimmy. But, all attempts failed, because Jack didn't tell him how wonderful he was and did not dish out admiration and attention constantly. When Jack did not inflate Jimmy's balloon with admiration and attention, Jimmy just stepped up his condemnation, castigation, fault- finding of him and his family.

Finally, Jack realized that Jimmy was toxic to him and his family and he rejected all the negative comments, deleted them from his mind and moved on. And still to this day they don't speak or interact with each other. Interacting with his brother was poisonous to his family, and Jack had to remove him from his circle of interaction even though he was family. It was the only way Jack could have joy, peace and healing for his wife and child.

On a positive note, in Jacks life he loved more than life, three women, his mom, his mother in law and his wife Ann. He adored all three. They loved Jack and he loved them. First, his mother in law had a business making a special lustrous shampoo for woman who dyed their hair. The special ingredients brought back luster to the damaged dyed hair. Marilyn Monroe used this same shampoo. His mother-in-law turned the business and the secret formula over to Jack.

When Jack and Ann sold the parents' home after his in laws passed, the man who bought the house thought the secret formula for the shampoo and equipment went with the sale of the house. But Jack refused to give it to him. He still has that secret formula.

Lovingly, Jack remembers one time going to a Yankee ball game with his mother- in- law. She yelled unmercifully at Ted Williams, taunting him because he was playing a lousy game. He came over to his mother in law and said, "Lady go home and take care of your grandkids".

Surprisingly, his mother-in-law bought Jack a college style Glen Falls High School ring that he fell in love with. He wore it every day. Overtime the stone became cracked so he bought a rainbow topaz and had the jeweler put the topaz on the ring. He is so proud of that ring.

In fact, one time while on a cruise he showed a lady his ring with the brilliant rainbow topaz stone. She admired his stone asked what kind of stone it was. When they stopped at one of the ports the lady bought a rainbow topaz ring and thanked Jack for showing her his ring.

Expressly, he misses is mother-in-law so much and took her passing in 1984 with ovarian cancer awfully hard. In this case, his mother-in-law used Johnson and Johnson Baby Powder in her private area to keep the area dry and fresh for years. Thirty-five years later they connected Johnson Baby Powder with ovarian cancer. By that time, the statutes of limitations ran out and most hospitals discarded their ovarian tissues samples after ten years. So, there also was no proof they could show that she used the powder to file a claim against the company.

Secondly, Jack adored his mom. She was the most beautiful person in his eyes. Her face was so wholesome and angelic looking. She always protected him when he was in trouble with his father, and he protected her when his father was abusing his mom in the best way he knew how. They had an incredibly special bond. He survived his childhood because of his mom, as awful as it was.

In fact, she taught him how to sew and embroider him name on his shirts and athletic bags. These skills came in quite handy later in life as an adult. He was able to sew torn clothing and other torn items. He had a special spot in his heart for his mom. Her passing fell heavy on Jack's heart. It was painful for him not to have her around anymore. Every time he hears the song, *You Are the Wind Beneath My Wings*, he cries like a baby. It reminds him of his loving mom. They played this song at her funeral. There was never ever any doubt that his mom loved him dearly.

Lastly, he adored Ann his wife. He was so grateful that he married Ann. His life with her was wonderful. They worked hard to build a nice nest egg for their retirement. Jack did hours and hours of overtime to build the nest egg. Ann saved all her money and they lived off Jacks income. They put all of Ann's salary and their savings from Jacks earnings into an IRA in her name. That's what they were going to use when they retired. When Ann's parents died, she sold the house and put that money into the IRA too. They both envisioned a genuinely nice comfortable retirement.

At this time, Ann and Jack were in the highlight of their life with everything going so well at home and in their careers. They both worked hard and played hard having a great time. They were looking forward to an adventurous retirement filled with joy and happiness. They were so optimistic and hopeful for what the future retirement would bring to them.

In fact, as he looked backed on his childhood life, he was so grateful that he saw the light and he set a new standard by turning the tide by enlarging his vision. He no longer lived under the bondage of his horrid childhood. He no longer cared about how his defeated family was in the past. He took a stand to be the one who makes a difference and went beyond the old barriers. He refused to accept the victim mentality and refused to just accept whatever comes his way. He rejected being passive sitting back and settling for a life of mediocrity. He rose up and put an end to that mind set of defeat. He broke the negative cycle and became a champion in life.

Ann and Jack were a power couple rich in faith, happiness, and joy. They were madly in love with each other enjoying life to the fullest. This marriage for Jack was the highlight of his life. Finally, finding someone who loves him dearly, someone he trusts implicitly, and someone who was the best mother of his son.

Their lifestyle was filled with fun attending concerts, going to beach resorts, taking wonderful cruises, going to racetracks, having fun with many friends. It couldn't be any better for both of them. He enjoyed her cooking and she cooked for Jack with love. She made life for Jack so easy, so he could go to work and be the best employee possible at work. She was the most exceptional wife any husband could have. His choice in marrying Ann was a good one.

Tragically, all of this came to a screeching halt when Ann fell ill and had a stroke paralyzing her left side just before retirement. She was bit by an insect not known if it was a tick or a mosquito, but it caused encephalitis. Fluid collected on her brain causing her blood pressure to go out of control and she sustained a stroke leaving her with a left sided paralysis.

# 3

# Unexpected Tragedy Hits

Jack tried to take care of Ann at home but did not have the resources to pay for 24/7 nursing care, nor did he have the equipment needed to care for her. He lacked expertise in caring for her physical needs. He did build a ramp to get her wheelchair up the stairs and ordered a hospital bed, but he needed much more than that to care for Ann in the home. She required expert nursing care. She needed special mattresses to prevent skin breakdown. She needed to be turned every two hours to prevent pneumonia and skin breakdown. She needed special lifts to get her in and out of bed. She required a specialized wheelchair with special cushions to prevent skin breakdown and a bath chair, all of which was costly.

While at home Jack was summoned by his wife every hour day and night to provide something she wanted or needed. It became painfully clear to him that he was not able to care for her by himself at home. He had to place her in a local nursing home.

However, this ate up the IRA in her name with their life savings. She and Jack found this difficult to accept. They both were severely depressed. He visited her twice a day everyday rain or shine. He was devastated at losing the wife he once had.

He learned that a portion of Ann's brain responsible for feeling joy was damaged and it was difficult for him to keep her spirits up. Although other parts of her brain were preserved thank God. She's smart and was able to carry on conversation with Jack without any major speech impediments. Despite these assets she wanted to die.

Explicitly, she had major mood swings and he never knew each day how she was going to greet him. One day she loved him; the next day she wanted divorce. Nothing he did satisfied her. He'd bring her videos, music, he tried to get her out in the car for a ride. Nothing appealed to her.

Due to the stroke, she was sarcastic, biting, insulting and intentionally hurtful. The changes in the brain from a stroke sometimes led to Ann behaving in ways that could be considered abusive. She lashed out at Jack when she was frustrated and took out her feelings on the one closest to her, Jack. She often was ready for a fight before Jack could even say hello. At times she was hateful, accusatory, and belligerent with Jack. She'd lose her temper over the most ridiculous things and threw tantrums.

It's important to know that caretakers like Jack must be very clear that they will not tolerate being verbally abused. The more the caretaker puts up with the maltreatment, the more they encourage the stroke victim to behave that way.

At times it was almost impossible to have a normal conversation with Ann because she would cut Jack off when he spoke. She brought up past issues and provoked arguments. It was her anger turned outward used to control Jack's behavior by causing him to feel guilty. Ann had so little in her environment that she could control. The only thing she could control was Jack. She felt safe deriding and ridiculing him because she knew he would not hurt her. Her insults hurt Jack. He felt worthless, like what he said made no difference, like he was a nobody. He began to feel responsible for the mistreatment.

Frequently, he was told by professionals that he was not doing himself any favors by putting up with this behavior. He needed to hold Ann to a certain standard of behavior and if he didn't, he was doing Ann an injustice, even though she had a stroke.

Sadly, Ann's moods broke Jack's heart. He knew it was the stroke that was responsible for the explosive outbursts and that it was not his wife's doing. It was so hard to see his wife who wouldn't say a bad word about anyone turn into a person at times he did not recognize. Even though he understood it was the stroke and the sense of loss she was experiencing that caused the caustic remarks, it was still hard for Jack to cope and deal with it.

Unfortunately, Ann had an inability to accept her losses. Ann insisted that Jack needed to take her home to care for her himself. His attempts to explain he does not have the resources or the expertise to care for her at home fell on deaf ears. She then would insult him and try to lay guilt trips on him for not taking her home. He left the home feeling guilty, defeated and lost. As she begged Jack to take her home his heart broke knowing he couldn't care for her at their home.

All attempts to work through Ann's feelings of loss and accept the limitations that have resulted have failed. Jack grieved the relationship he once had with Ann.

Under the circumstances, there were days where she was so bitter and angry that this happened to her that she'd threaten everyone in sight with calling the police to have everyone arrested. She wouldn't give anyone especially Jack a break from her rancorous, pugnacious attitude.

At times she needed constant attention and acted out to get it. It was a total nightmare for Jack. Ann was so frustrated, feeling helpless and feeling a total loss of control. So, to assert her autonomy she lashed out at Jack in an attempt to make him feel guilty. She was disparaging and disapproving with Jack in hopes of making him feel so bad that he'd go home feeling guilty.

Indeed, these guilt trips Ann placed on Jack were getting him down to say the least.

Another key point is that her stroke resulted in emotional impairment. Her distorted perception and view of what's really going on often resulted in inaccurate reports to Jack when he visited. She distorted at times what her care involved on any particular day. This upset Jack because he had difficulty sorting out what was real and what was distorted.

Sadly, she is totally dependent on the staff to change her position, manage her elimination needs, bath her, dress her, get her out of bed, feed her and brush her teeth. One day she'd have a warm caring aid take care of her that made all this tolerable, and the next she'd have an aid that was not supportive or friendly. This impacted significantly on her mood, anxiety and feeling of frustration and helplessness. It put a knife in Jack's heart on Ann's bad days. Jack was on a roller coaster with emotions up and down and all over the place.

Surprisingly, when Jack asked questions or expressed concern over the care Ann was receiving sometimes a crusty staff member became defensive and said to him well take her home and care for her yourself. Can you imagine having to deal with this attitude of some of the staff. Especially when he was paying handsomely to have Ann cared for. The depressing environment was bad enough, but to deal with arrogant, self-righteous, uncaring attitudes took a toll on Jack's emotional wellbeing.

Simultaneously, the two of them grieved over their former life. They were both painfully lonely and depressed. Jack missed Ann's interesting conversations, her home cooked meals, their travels together, and their intimacy. It was awful living without his beloved wife as he knew her before her illness. Ann missed her trips to Virginia Beach and her cruises. She missed being in the arms of her loved one Jack. They both missed the warm intimate relationship they once enjoyed. The two of them have suffered enormously.

Happily, there were some patients in the home Ann bonded with. She became friends with a special needs man in his fifties with Cerebral

Palsy. Every now and then they had a little therapy dog come into the home that she loved to hug. One of the high school volunteers named Megan took a special interest in Ann. Megan's visits lifted Ann's spirits and she looked forward to the days when Megan volunteered.

Moreover, on occasion some of the staff brought in their young children and put them in the creative arts room where they painted. Ann loved when the children came in. She also bonded with a priest Father Carlos. But soon learned that he was accused of sexual abuse and was no longer part of the local parish. She was devastated with this news.

In light of this situation Jack began to look around the nursing home and wondered if this was going to be his fate. He was becoming very depressed more and more socially isolated. He had no friends to talk with. His whole day evolved going to the home advocating for Ann, making sure she was being cared for properly, but all this was taking a serious effect on his physical and mental wellbeing.

In reality, when he wasn't at the home, he was dealing with an extremely negative woman in Social Services trying to get the benefits Ann was entitled to. It was a nightmare for him. The process was so complicated and difficult to navigate, and it wore him down to a frazzle. The woman he dealt with displayed no compassion, empathy, or concern for his situation. He dreaded dealing with that department and that woman.

At the same time, he was so saddened to see their life savings being totally wiped out. The little nest egg they both saved and put in an IRA in Ann's name for retirement was being flushed away. This was driving Jack crazy and more and more depressed. With their life savings being devoured by the nursing home Jack was barely making it financially. He was eating spam and sardines that he bought in the dollar store. He had to be very frugal so he would be able to buy gas money and enough to handle any car repairs so he could visit Ann each day.

Then again, to make matters worse his bank closed, and he had to transfer all his accounts to another bank. The transfer was delayed, and he ended up not having enough money in the checking to pay his bills. His pension check and Social Security check got caught up in the process and they delayed getting his assets to the new bank. This created intense anxiety for Jack because he took pride in being debt free and always paying his bills on time.

Finally, he expressed concern to his son about the banking issue and his wonderful son stepped up to the plate and deposited a sum of money in the new checking to take care of things till all the transfers took place. Jack and his son had a relationship that any dad and son would give their right arm to have. They both loved each other dearly.

Once again Jack expressed how proud of his son he was and reveled in the fact that even as a child he was never a bit of problem. He was always a warm, loving child that was just a nice person. Jack took great pride in raising a wonderful child. He and Ann made sacrifices to provide for him, sacrifices other parents often are not willing to make. Their relationship father and son is a relationship that many children do not experience. Jack, Jr. knows the sacrifices his parents made for him and he is incredibly grateful to them. The one silver lining in all this tragedy for Jack, Sr. is the relationship that he has with his son. It's the one thing that keeps Jack moving forward.

Indeed, all this stress of dealing with social services, the bank transfer, the financial straits he finds himself in, the nursing home issues and Ann's condition, Jack was becoming a boring person. He was obsessed with all the negativities surrounding Ann's illness that he was no longer able to feel any joy in life. Not only did the illness take Ann's life, but it took Jack's life as well. Life was miserable. Jack struggled with his anger toward God and wondered why God dealt them a horrific blow. His diminished faith made his hope dim and his purpose in life totally blurred.

At this time, the only thing both looked forward to in the home were the holiday celebrations. Activity directors and volunteers all came in dressed for the specific holiday. On St. Patti's day they had corned beef and cabbage, had Irish dancers and music. It was very festive. Jack bought Ann a green stoned bracelet for the occasion that lifted her spirits. On Memorial Day and the Fourth of July, they had patriotic music and barbequed spareribs. Ann wore her mother's patriotic medal and her father's dog tags on these occasions with pride. They celebrated Christmas, Thanksgiving, New years and Halloween in grand style too.

However, once the holiday was over it was business as usual. A very depressing environment with little to look forward to. Both Ann and Jack were stuck in Plato's cave with no insight or plan to escape.

In fact, Jack was emotionally drained. His anxiety was increased as he worried about Ann's wellbeing. He felt he had to be there constantly or else she wouldn't get proper care, meals, or they wouldn't make her comfortable, or they wouldn't be nice to her. It was so frustrating for him to deal with some staff that obviously hated their job and were surly and didn't care for the patients properly. When he brought some issues to the staff's attention some would become defensive and blew him off. All of this weighed heavy on Jack's heart.

Unfortunately, negative self-talk starting creeping into his mind again. Thoughts of anger, anxiety, fear, insecurity, lack of self-confidence were taking up valuable space in his mind. Each day he dwelled on his losses and found it difficult to delete them from his mind. He was obsessed with the negativity of losing his wife as he knew her, the nursing home environment, his financial losses, the uncaring staff, and it was taking a severely injuring his emotional health. He became isolated and lonely. He had no sense of joy, happiness, or peace of mind. This was a wretched situation for both Jack and Ann.

Sadly, Jack's whole life dwelled on the grief-stricken, sorrowful, inconsolable situation of Ann's illness. He was unable to focus on anything else, but the bad deal they were dealt. They were both miserable and saw no future for themselves. Over and over again the broken record played in Jack' mind: we got dealt a bad deal, will the money last to care for Ann, dealing with that lady in Social Services is a nightmare, will I have enough gas money to visit her, the staff are uncaring, Ann wants to die, Ann wants to come home, I miss my former life.

His life is filled with anger, bitterness, and anxiety. These poisoning, continuous thoughts are killing Jack. His life was totally consumed with the nursing home and financial issues. He can't sleep at night. At 4AM he's up wandering around in a state of panic.

Not to mention, when Jack returned home after his visit with Ann in the nursing home, he found it hard to go into his own house because his wife was not there to greet him. He no longer had the wonderful home cooked meals. The intimacy once enjoyed was gone. He lies in bed by himself lonely and depressed, severely lacking tactile stimulation.

Explicitly, he was surrounded by medical equipment that he secured when he tried to take care of her at home. All the medical equipment reminded him constantly of the losses they sustained.

Furthermore, her shoes, purses, and clothes were in sight for him to see that made him sad. Her clothing and high heels reminded him of the good times they had that were now nonexistent.

Moreover, boxes and boxes of receipts, pay stubs, check books, cancelled checks from year one were all over the house that Ann took care of. All these boxes reminded him of how she took care of the bills and just reinforced his lack of ability to keep up with that.

Thus, the house was so cluttered it was closing in on him. It hadn't been cleaned in seven years. Living in the cluttered home was more than he could bear. To make matters worse, Ann forbid him to get rid of the medical equipment and her shoes, dresses, paperwork and items, making him feel guilty if he cleaned out the house.

In light of this, his solution with all the negative reminders of their situation inside the house was to live in his car all day and only go in the house when he wanted to go to bed, thereby avoiding all the negative reminders. He did this for seven years. Living in total misery.

Thus, he took to living in the car till the neighbors became concerned. They thought it was odd for him to be in his car all evening. On two occasions a neighbor called the police to check on him. The first time the neighbor was thinking he was ill or dead in the car. The other time because his radio was very loud since Jack is severely deaf. The police came by and said why are you sitting in your car? Jack replied by saying I'm listening to my radio, is it a crime to sit in my car on my own property? And they said" no". And finally, they left.

Significantly, one night as Jack was going into the house to sleep, he tripped on his shoelace, his knee gave out and down he went in the driveway. Unable to get up because he had nothing to grab on to, he crawled back to his car grabbed onto the car door handle and got in the car to get warmed up. He knew he'd freeze to death in the cold night if he didn't get into his car. He was unable to walk into the house since he was in so much pain, but was able to crawl to his car. After he gained his composure and warmed himself up, he struggled to walk back inside the house. His knee and hip were extremely painful.

Considering this, the next day he couldn't get out of bed he was in so much pain. He called the nursing home to tell them he wouldn't be visiting Ann that day. First time in seven years he missed a visit with his wife. The next day he couldn't walk well and stayed home again. And the third day he stayed home also.

Since, the neighbors didn't see him for three days and the car wasn't moved in three days they became concerned. So, they called the police again to see if he was dead. Now the police were inquiring why he wasn't in the car. Jack reassured them he was fine and after a half hour the police finally left.

At this point, Jack called his son and said the police first come because I'm sitting in my car for long periods listening to the radio and then they come because I'm not sitting in the car.

Thus, to solve the problem of the neighbors concern he gave all his concerned neighbors his phone number and asked them to please call him if they have a concern.

Important to realize, Jack went from being on cloud nine happy as can be to the bottom of the cliff wallowing around in self-pity, misery, bitterness, and anger. He sees no way out, has no vision on how he can turn this around, has no vision on how to rise up over this defeat and has no idea how to free himself from this bondage. He has resigned himself to living a life in constant turmoil, always facing some challenge from keeping him from being happy, living with a victim mentality, a mindset of defeat and living a life of mediocrity.

During his entire years of marriage his wife made all the decisions related to maintenance of home, financial issues, paying the bills, banking issues, what they bought, where they went on vacation .All Jack had to do was go to work and bring the check home and hand it over to Ann to do what needed to be done.

When his wife could no longer do any of that he found himself having to make all those decisions on his own. He was totally out of his comfort zone and had to learn how to do all that for the first time in over fifty years. It was very anxiety provoking for him to say the least. He felt so overwhelmed and stressed out.

In fact, the only silver lining amongst this tragedy was his brother in law and one sister Ellen. The two of them gave him something to take hold of, a lifeline and they were his anchor at his exceptionally low times. His sister Ellen was so understanding, listened, offered support and was always there for him. He found Ellen so helpful and emotionally uplifting when he interacted with her. These two people Ellen and his brother- in- law were the only ones in his life that he interacted with in a positive manner during this terrible crisis.

The one person who kept Jack going was Ellen. She checked on him frequently offing emotional support, offered advice and was a great listener. He relied on her to cheer him up and she was always there for him. She was a true saint. He often said he wouldn't know what to do if it wasn't for her support over the years. Her husband John was terrific too. Jack always like John and enjoyed interacting with him. He had a lot of respect for John and how hard he worked and loved listening to his work stories. These two people saved Jack from total madness.

By all means interacting with his other younger sister Audrey was another story. She made him even more depressed. She was married to a loser who didn't work, woke up at noon and ate potato chips all day.

His sister was a brittle diabetic, had blood in her urine, had kidney dysfunction, had severe cataracts, and couldn't see anything. She didn't have enough money to put gas in the car to drive to the doctor's office. She was unable work. Their house finally went into foreclosure.

Under the circumstances, Jack is in no position to help. He in the past paid for their winter gas bill and sent money to them to get them through tough times. She began to see him as an ATM machine and began to expect the help. But now the nursing home ate up his entire life's savings to care for his wife Ann, and he himself was surviving on sardines and spam from the dollar store. He was no longer able to offer financial assistance to his sister.

In reality, he accepted his life as just barely surviving and always focusing on problems and fretting about obstacles. Jack's life had absolutely no quality to it. His outlook was bleak.

Interestingly, Dr. Susan McMillan's research on caregivers cited in *Appendix A* reminds us that the highly stressed caregiver has been found to be at increased risk for depression, health care problems and increased mortality rates. Such caregivers experience high levels of burden due to intense psychological, physical, and economic strain, face not only stresses of caregiving, but the potential loss of the loved one.

In fact, caregiving takes an enormous toll on a caregiver's quality of life. The caregiver's mood, worry, sleep, daily life, family life, socialization and other dimensions are all impacted negatively as it relates to quality of life. Both the patient and the caregiver must struggle to adjust and respond to the demands of the threat. It's not surprising that the spouses experience as much if not more distress than the patients.

Thus, the distress that the caregiver experiences not only may affect their ability to care for their loved one but may also impact on their ability to provide emotional support needed for patient to participate in activities of daily living and other physical aspects of care.

Often, the stress of caregiving creates a strain on the marital relationship. Economic future, financial strain, disruption of sleep, maintaining outside activities, outlook on life, spirituality, mental strain, guilt, frustration, nervousness, eating habits all take a huge toll on the caregiver. Caregiver neuroticism of focusing on negative aspects of caregiving, feeling inadequate and failure in all things in life, resigning oneself to accepting there's no way out is quite common among caregivers.

Indeed, Jack experienced all these dreadful effects of caregiving reported in the research conducted by Dr. Mc Millan. He led a wretched life of misery and misfortune plagued with hardship, suffering, anxiety, torment, deprivation, pain, sorrow. He had no vision on how to improve his situation. He engulfed himself in guilt and anger feeling all alone cocooned in Plato's Cave chained up in a world on bondage. He led a life of misery.

# 4

# Failed Attempt to Escape Bonds of Guilt & Anger

**Plato's cave story** reminds us of Jack. Since his wife's tragic illness, he was a prisoner in the cave. His whole perception of realty was the nursing home. He was chained to the nursing home feeling guilty if he had any fun, because Ann could not participate. He felt it would be selfish of him to have some fun. He was socially isolated, never went anywhere or did anything except listen to his radio and read a history book. He did this sitting in his car till it was time to go to bed. He was like the prisoners in the cave who refused to come out. He marinated in his misery, self-pity, and anger.

Over time, he became boring to Ann with no new stories to share. His demeanor was depressed and all he could talk about was the issues he was having with Social Services and their financial difficulties. He was obsessed with the fact their life savings from her folks' home and her salary and Social Security were taken over by the nursing home. All he kept saying was Ann we were dealt a bad deal and dwelled on that every day. He lacked energy, vibrancy, was unable to feel any sense of joy. His whole perceived reality was the dreadful nursing home. He was immersed in his misery and was not helpful in lifting Ann's spirits.

At this instant, Joel Osteen a motivational author and speaker was on the radio while Jack was listening. He inspired Jack to make attempts to come out of the cave. He heard Joel Osteen share a story about a little frog that was born at the bottom of a well.

Apparently, this frog was content swimming in the water, content with a life of status quo and mediocrity in the bottom of the well. He thought I feel safe here at the bottom of the well living in a narrow-limited mindset. One day he looked up and saw the light at the top and wondered what was up there and climbed to the top. He peeked out and saw a pond. He couldn't believe it. It was so much larger than the bottom of the well. He ventured out further and saw a huge lake.

As he hopped along outside the well, he and came across an ocean. He couldn't believe his eyes. He saw water everywhere. Totally shocked he realized there's a whole new world out there and that he limited his thinking for so long. He saw that life was so much bigger and greater than he imagined.

While listening to the story Jack wondered if he was like that little frog enclosed in his little well. Living with the status quo, mediocrity with resentment seething below the surface of every conversation about the bad deal he was dealt, his life savings flushed away, dwelling on the pains of his wife's illness, imprisoned in the well in defeat.

Eventually, he talked with a friend of his and she told him he needed to make attempts to come out of the cave and the well to bring some joy back in his life. She said how many years do you think you have left. Ten if you're incredibly lucky? She encouraged him to take all those negative feelings of fear, lack of trust, anger, emotional confusion, emotional chaos, anxiety, guilt, and isolation and throw them down the bathtub drain and say get out of my mind. You are no longer going to occupy valuable space in my mind. I'm done with you and I am going to move on.

At the same time, his friend told him he would be so much more of support to Ann, which was his main goal, if he'd get out and interact with people, do fun things with others and become more excited about life. By bringing some joy into his life he would pass that on to Ann. He would have some funny stories to tell her, he'd be more vibrant, less depressed, and more fun to be with when he visited Ann. He had to leave all the negative garbage about social services and financial issues he was bombarding Ann with out of his visits.

Jack needed to escape from the cave and the well that had him chained down in misery. His friend helped him develop an initial implementation plan.

**IMPLEMENTATION PLAN:**

- Realize that by getting out of the cave and the well you will be more of a support to Ann. Your visits will be filled with energy positive stories and will bring excitement to her.
- Say to yourself every morning I can do this, I'm intelligent, inspired, and willing to exert the energy it requires to take the initiative to get out with people. I'm not being selfish by having some fun. I will not feel guilty having fun. Having fun will help lift Ann's spirits. I will not let these negative feelings occupy valuable real estate in my head. My head is my house so get the hell out.
- Call Justin his friend and say the next time you go play golf I'd like to join you.
- Call Rocco Polo his old Varsity Basketball Coach and say let's go to breakfast. Say to coach I don't have anything special to talk about I just need to get out.
- Go to your upcoming reunion. The fee is expensive, but fork it up and go.

Indeed, this was a start to escape the cave and well. He took these baby steps to get out a bit, and although it was difficult for him to do, he tried to do it to his credit. He worked on developing the courage to move out of his comfort zone. His major assets were that he had a heart filled with love, ears that listened and a hand that was always ready to help. He had a can-do attitude and a never give up mindset that he learned from his Coach Rocco Polo. But all these assets were stuck in mud because he was chained in the cave. He just needed some help to gain the insight how much better he could support Ann if he developed the courage to escape from the cave and escape the bonds that held him in the cave.

Without delay, he took one day at a time one step forward, two steps backward. This went on for several months. He talked more often with Coach Polo. Finally, he met with Coach Polo and called him periodically to talk about how the New York Yankees were doing. This meeting brought new energy into his soul. They are both Yankee fans and both were pitchers in their day, and they had a lot to talk about.

Likewise, he called his friend Justin and told him the next time he plays golf he'd like to join him. This was hard for Jack to do. He wasn't accustomed to inviting himself to activities with anyone. He received several invitations to play golf, but each time Jack declined, because he claimed had other things to do.

In preparation, of playing golf he planned to go the range to practice so he wouldn't look ridiculous on the golf course, since it was awhile since he played golf. He didn't want to look like a fool on the green when he finally played golf.

Meanwhile, he worked hard to get the negative thoughts out of his mind a big part of the implementation plan. The next big test for Jack was developing the courage to go to the Glen Falls High School reunion where he'd see lots of old high school friends.

Specifically, he began working on developing the courage to embrace the three C's. He tried to make a CHOICE to escape from the cave, he took the CHANCE and he is trying to CHANGE his mindset. But he's not there yet and has a lot more work to do to get there.

Under these circumstances, his friend Mary pointed out to him that the emotional chains of fear, lack of trust, anger, bitterness, fear of abandonment, emotional confusion, fear of authority, emotional chaos, anxiety, guilt, social isolation were all related to low self-esteem that was developed during his childhood were resurfacing again.

Expressly, she told Jack that by dwelling on all the negative aspects of his wife's illness such as my life savings being eaten up by the nursing home, social services is a nightmare for me to deal with, the staff are uncaring, the nursing home food is lousy, I'm in financial straits, I miss my wife as I knew her, were taking a stronghold on him preventing him from reaching his destiny. He had to shake off his self-pity.

To clarify, Mary pointed out that he was engaged in negative self-talk. I'm not interesting, I'm not smart, I'm not worthy, I'm have nothing to offer others, I don't fit in with others, I'm not talented, I'm not creative, I'll never turn this nursing home around. He reinforced his negative thoughts and negative self-talk that he had nothing to offer.

Also, she told him that he doesn't see how amazing he is. She said you are amazing person who was talented, smart, interesting, creative, strong, confident, disciplined focused and qualified. You just don't believe it.

Indeed, Jack was suffering from complicated prolonged grief with the loss of the relationship he once had with Ann. His grief was so profound it interfered with Jack' ability to move forward with his own life. He was displaying the following signs:

- He felt he had no purpose anymore
- He had difficulty performing activities such as working with social services, his banking issues and chores as shopping and doing laundry.
- Experiencing continued feelings of guilt blaming himself for not seeing that her illness needed attention. Feeling guilty that he was well, and she wasn't.
- Wishing it were him that was sick instead of his wife

- Losing all desire to socialize
- Feeling like he didn't fit in with others. It was awkward for him to go to parties, reunions and get togethers.

By all means, he couldn't get past all this to create a new fulfilling life that had purpose. Losing the relationship, he once had with his wife was devastating. He felt numb, shocked, brokenhearted, and anxious. At times he felt anger toward his wife for not seeking treatment when she knew she was ill. The grief was causing detriment to his health. He wasn't sleeping well, eating properly, or exercising. He had no energy was feeling anxious, highly stressed and void of any sense of joy.

Clearly, it was apparent, that Jack needed to quit rehashing over and over in his mind the negative aspects of his wife's illness and had to start working on rejecting all the negative emotional chains that have him bound in defeat. Mary wrote the following poem for Jack.

### Escape the Cave

*Come out of Plato's Cave*
*To regain a joyful life*
*And free your mind from all the strife*

*You suffered enough my friend*
*Feel the gift of joy again*
*Let the healing sink in to allow you to transcend*

*The joy, high spirits, and humor you see in me*
*I want for you so you can see*
*A new life that's carefree*

*Bring into your life some pizzazz*
*Shine like a rainbow topaz*
*Fall in love with life again*
*For the years that remain*

Then again, the issue of him not being able to live in the house came up with Jack and Mary. Jack continued to engage himself in his self-pity party obsessing with how lonely he was and how he couldn't bear to go into his own house without Ann greeting him with a warm smile and a big hug.

Specifically, he dwelled on how depressed he felt when he looked around the house, and saw Ann's items that she loved, and how he missed so much the two of them enjoying their evening talks. When his eyes glanced at the medical equipment, she utilized when he tried to care for her at home such as the commode, wheelchair, hospital bed, diapers, and bed pads it reinforced the bad deal he and Ann were dealt. It brought up negative thoughts and anger began to emerge.

Moreover, when he went into their bedroom and saw her high heels and clothes, it brought back memories of the good times, they had on their cruises dancing and dining that are now gone forever and he began to feel hopelessly sad.

Additionally, the house filled with multiple boxes of paperwork still in the house for seven years reinforced how difficult it was for him to manage all the bills, banking and taxes that Ann always took care of. Feelings of anxiety overwhelmed him.

Markedly, his house was like a living shrine of his wife reminding him of the good times he and his wife experienced that are gone forever.

Painfully, the home was so cluttered with the past that it became a negative astounding paralyzing emotional experience for him, making it impossible for him to go into the house. After visiting Ann, he drove to his house and took refuge in his car.

Chiefly, he stayed in his car reading, listening to music, and his beloved Yankee games when they played ball. He kept special mementos is his car that gave him comfort. His car was his cocooned sanctuary. He didn't go back into the house till late at night when it was time to sleep. This went on for seven years ever since Ann's illness.

Indeed, it was a pathetic, sad existence he was living. There was no quality of life for Jack and was an extreme awful situation. It was an unhealthy situation physically and emotionally.

Despite much prodding from Mary for him to go into his house and listen to the radio on his couch he refused to go in till it was time to go to sleep. Mary explained to him that after seven years this was totally out of the ordinary and was aberrant behavior. She told him he was holding himself hostage to all the clutter in the house and he was being held in bondage by guilt of throwing out or donating the stuff. Her words fell on deaf ears and he continued to stay in his car till it was bedtime.

Surely, attempts to get Jack out the cave was not going well. He never got out to play golf with Justin, he never went out to practice his golf shots, and he never attended his High School reunion. The implementation plans fell flat on its face. Mary knew she needed to do something else to get him out of the cave. Something big had to happen to loosen the bondage chains that shackled him.

Meanwhile, Mary suggested he attend a support group of men and woman who had spouses that had a stroke. The support groups closest to him were given to him, and he came up with the excuse it's too far to drive. Mary said you're not going because it's not held in your back yard. He resisted and said he didn't feel comfortable talking about his troubles with strangers. So, Mary cut him some slack and backed off.

In fact, the next day Mary spent all day on the phone with the Office of Aging trying to locate a person who could share with Jack what free benefits they offered the elderly that may appeal to him and that Jack may be eligible to receive. She finally connected with a young woman who was genuinely nice and said she'd be happy to come to Jack's home to conduct an interview with him. The woman explained that part of the visit included a home assessment for fall risks. They look for clutter in the walking pathways, scattered rugs that may slide and other areas for potential fall risks. Often when elderly people fall and hit their head or break a hip they never recover and circle the drain to death.

Also, they assess the cleanliness of the home such as dishes stacked in the sink with roaches crawling around, rodent infestation and anything that may create a health hazard such as lack of fire alarms, etc.

Additionally, they look for disrepair on the outside of the house since they have services to help elderly to repair such things as siding falling off, and other obvious disrepair issues.

So, Mary gave Jack the woman's number to call. He called the woman and she told him she wanted to do an interview with him at his home. He told her he wanted the interview to take place in his wife's Nursing Home. When she said the interview had to be done in his home, he lost interest. She asked how he was coping with his wife's stroke thinking he may benefit from some free professional counseling and he said he was coming along by reading Joel Osteen books and by talking with his friend Mary. She asked him if he gave money to Joel Osteen and that infuriated him.

In all fairness to her she was probably just trying to assess if he was a victim of a scam. Often the elderly are taken advantage of by religious groups. He reassured her he gave no money to Joel Osteen and told her that all he needed was his friend Mary and Joel Osteen's inspiring words and wasn't interested.

At this point, Mary was trying everything she could think of to help Jack to resolve his prolonged grief and his miserable living conditions. But his lack of trust in people and agencies, his stubbornness and hardheadedness were preventing him from accepting help and thus moving forward.

However, Mary felt as though God was using her to grate against Jack like sandpaper to rub off the rough edges of stubbornness, bullheadedness, and the lack of trust he had to move Jack to the next level. She believed it was a mini trial put in place to test Jack and to bring light to these impurities in his character. She was trying to reveal to Jack areas where he needed to change. But this trial failed and thus he was not toughened up to reach his next level. He chose to run away from the trial because it was uncomfortable and not convenient. Mary did not give up on him, however.

For sure, Jack wasn't making significant progress but kept saying to Mary I'm trying. He sent Mary several texts that began to concern Mary. The texts said, "Don't give up on me I need you". "Hope you're feeling better I need you". "Don't get bit by a shark while you're on vacation I need you".

At this point, Mary began to be concerned that Jack was becoming too dependent on her and wondered if she was being helpful or harmful to Jack. Not being a psychologist and was just a good friend she prayed to God for signs that He wanted her to continue to work with Jack.

Consequently, she discussed her concerns with her husband asking him if he thought she was a little too much involved with Jack and did he think she was interacting too much with Jack. Her husband said you do interact with him a lot, maybe so.

As a result, Mary reflected in a quiet area and started thinking of what to say to Jack about the situation. Mary came up with something and shared it with her husband and he responded, "Well if he's in that bad of a place and you can help him go ahead and continue and reassess later".

Then, she continued to ask God to guide her steps and direct her in the right path. She was willing to work hard to help Jack as long as it was therapeutic and not harmful to him. She began to get thoughts and a gut feeling that this was a task that God had in mind for her to do, so she continued the journey with Jack.

# 5

# DITCHING THE CHAINS, DEMONS AND ENEMIES

MARY CONTINUED TO work with Jack lending him support, kindness and encouragement. Mary shared a book with Jack entitled ***The Power of I AM*** by Joel Osteen. This book turned Oprah Winfrey's life around and Mary found it extremely helpful too. She encouraged Jack to read it. She hoped it would help him come out of the cave, help him ditch the demons and eventually bring joy, happiness, and peace back to his heart.

In fact, she felt confident if he read that book and three others ***Think Better Live Better, You Can and You Will, and Your Best Life Now***, he could bring back his life feeling joy, happiness and fulfilled once again by thinking more positively and eliminating all the negative thoughts that have dominated his entire life. As long as he was motivated to read the books and willing to accept feedback and make the necessary changes in his life Mary was more than willing to work with Jack.

Surprisingly, he was open to reading the books and in fact he was very motivated. He accepted verbal feedback well from Mary even when it was slightly unpleasant. He never became defensive or argumentative. In fact, he was like a sponge soaking up everything Mary said.

Thus, he started reading the books with delight, enthusiasm, and excitement. He actually loved them. The books opened a new whole world to him. He could see himself in many of Joel Osteen's examples. It was like the light bulb turned on and it gave him many "Ah Ha" moments.

In fact, Jack learned by reading ***Your Best Life Now*** one will never go beyond the barriers of their mind if we continue to think we can't do something. He read that if we think we can't do something, then we never will. If we are defeated in our mind, we have already lost the battle. If we don't think we can rise up and set a new standard, it's not going to happen. The barrier is in our mind. That's what scripture calls a stronghold. It's a wrong thinking pattern that keeps us imprisoned in defeat. That's why it is so important we think positive thoughts of hope, faith, and victory. Reading that made quite a positive impression on him.

Explicitly, after reading this book he realized that instead of going forward with attitude of faith, expecting good things, he was going around with a poor defeated mentality. Around and around he went, focusing on problems, always complaining, fretting about obstacles standing between him and his destiny. This insight was huge for Jack.

Prior to reading the books he was dwelling on the pains associated with his wife's illness. It became acutely clear to him that his self-talk was comprised of thoughts I'm never going to be able to deal with social services, they are impossible to work with, my life's savings is going to the nursing home, I'll never make it financially, my wife and I were dealt a bad deal, why us? It's not fair. I'm so lonely, I'll never feel peace or joy again. The nursing home is not taking good care of my wife, even with all the money they get from us. I'll never be able to have fun again, it's not fair to my wife, I'd feel guilty if I had fun. He was submersing in his misery, self-pity, anger, guilt, and anxiety.

Surprisingly, after reading this book, Jack was jolted out of his complacency. He realized he was lingering in misery long enough. He recognized he had to do a new thing in his life. He was not going to let this situation determine how he was going to live his last years of life.

Markedly, he comprehended that his thinking was keeping him imprisoned in defeat. He began to see and understand that he was immersed in his problems long enough. He knew it was time to move on, to let go of his loneliness, his pain in losing his wife as she once was, and feelings of insecurity in dealing with social services and his anger over losing his life's savings.

Finally, he was inspired to develop a fresh vison for his life and became fully aware that he had about ten years left God willing. He grasped the fact that he couldn't continue in his victim mentality and expect to live in victory. Likewise, he knew he couldn't live in a perpetual pity party and have his situation improve in his life. He wasn't satisfied with where he was in his life.

In fact, he learned that life is to short not to enjoy each and single day. Expressly, he learned that happiness is a decision he makes. He knew there are days when bad things happen, or things don't turn out as expected. But he was determined to decide that he's going to be happy despite his circumstances. He's going to be happy despite the bad days.

However, one of the most difficult challenged for Jack was dealing with the guilt associated with Ann's bad moods. Jack was told to be noticeably clear with Ann that he will not tolerate being verbally abused. The more the Jack puts up with the maltreatment, the more he encouraged Ann to behave that way.

Clearly, he began to understand more fully that because Ann was paralyzed, she had no control of her environment. It was very frustrating for her. The only thing she had control over was Jack. She made him feel guilty by her outburst of hurtful comments that she verbalized to Jack. She knew Jack would not hurt her, and so she felt safe deriding him unmercifully. He finally accepted the fact that his relationship with Ann that he once had was gone and her bad moods were all she had to control. He remained calm, and peaceable even though Ann was not.

In the final analysis, he recognized her behavior was a result of the stroke. Understanding the reasons for her lashing out at him made it overtime easier for him to disengage from and no longer felt guilty. Ann's verbal lashings no longer have the power to hurt him. The name calling, anger and insults thrown his way now no longer hurts Jack as much. This was the most difficult obstacle he had to overcome to get his life back.

Surprisingly, all the emotional chains that led to the fundamental problem of low self-esteem and lack of confidence started coming off and his thinking of not seeing himself highly was being replaced by positive thinking. He began to see himself as great and began seeing his own extraordinary qualities. He focused each day on the things he was thankful for and deleted all the negative labels that Ann put on him.

Accordingly, Joel Osteen reminded him of scripture that says, "Strip off the old nature and put on the new man." It says, "Be constantly renewed in the spirit of your mind, having a fresh mental and spiritual attitude." Joel reminded Jack that he can't just sit back and expect the new man to appear. Nor can he go through life focusing on the negative aspects of life and expect things to get better. Jack knew he had to ditch the negative thoughts and demons and embrace a fresh new attitude. He changed his thought patterns and started concentrating on the good things and the good blessings he has. As you think in your heart and mind so you will become.

Meanwhile, he reflected on Joel's words and made a list of all the things he was thankful for. He was encouraged to think of them every day and especially on days when Ann was is one of her foul moods.

**THIS WAS JACK'S LIST OF THANKFUL THINGS:**

- Thankful my wife is alive
- Thankful I'm able to cope
- Thankful I'm not in debt
- Thankful my house is now in my son's name
- Thankful my friend wrote a great book
- Thankful my friend didn't get eaten by shark while on vacation
- Thankful that my car is payed for
- Thankful I have a successful son who loves me dearly
- Thankful I have a goal to write a book
- Thankful for my wife's care
- Thankful my wife loves me
- Thankful he reunited with Mary
- Thankful his son, daughter in law and animals are OK
- Thankful I'm a great father with wisdom and wise advice
- Thankful I have a great sister Ellen and brother in law
- Thankful I have three trusted friends
- Thankful for the many mercies God showed me
- Thankful I found my passion to write poems, songs and draw sketches.

At this time, he started renewing his faith and accepted that God is in charge, God will renew him, he thought. He began to think and pray big. He practiced thinking of his list of things he was thankful for every day and during his visits with Ann to flood his mind with positive thoughts. Eventually there was no more room in his mind for negative thoughts or attacks.

Hence, when he came in to visit Ann and she was in one of her bad moods even if she cried, he put his foot down and said to himself, I'm not going to let this bad mood take my peace. I'm going to rule over my emotions. I'm not going to allow myself to get upset and aggravated. I'm going to choose to be happy.

Forthwith, he learned we are a mist, a vapor, we're here for the moment and then were gone. Life is flying by, so he decided he wasn't going to waste another moment of his precious time being upset, hurt, worried or feeling guilty. He said to himself no other person can make me happy; I must learn how to be happy within myself. He was empathetic to Ann, was calm and peaceable when she was in a wicked mood. But now he didn't let it steal his happiness. He gave himself permission to say to himself I'm not going to let Ann's poor mood impact on my day or peace. This was an extraordinary accomplishment for Jack.

In essence, the next biggest challenge was dealing with the frustration and anger of the nursing home. He continued to think constantly how awful the nursing home was: the food was not good, some of the staff are unfriendly and don't like their job, we're paying 350 dollars a day for this care, I could put her on cruise for one solid year and it wouldn't cost this much, she has to wait till her roommate gets a bath before they give Ann one, and on and on. Instead of all the negative rubbish he started focusing all the positive aspects the nursing home offered his wife.

Specifically, he focused on the fact that the home provided the specialized care Ann needs that he could not provide. Hence, he began to appreciate that the home had Physical Therapy, Occupational Therapy, they had ready access to a Nurse Practitioner, MD generalists and specialists in area of wound management, psychiatry so when problems arouse in any area in the middle of the night or day he did not have to deal with it. The home had access to all the help she may need, and he could be free of worry.

Likewise, he began to value the youth volunteers that came to give Ann a shot in the arm when they visited her. They had therapy dog that Ann loved interreacting with. The home was clean; the food was nutritious, not great cruise food, but not bad.

Additionally, the home had an activities department that planned special Friday night happy hours where each resident could partake in one glass of wine or one beer and for those that did not want a fancy drink, they had sparkling water and root beer. They made the evening festive and fun.

Moreover, every holiday was celebrated in grand fashion and gave Ann something to look forward to. Christmas, Easter, St. Patrick's Day, Fourth of July, Memorial Day, Thanksgiving, New Year's Eve and Day, Birthdays, Anniversaries, Labor Day, and Octoberfest were all celebrated at the home. Ann wore her dad and grandfather's military medals on the patriotic celebrations and, Jack brought in a special gift for the other holidays such as a green bracelet for St. Patrick's Day, and a turquoise necklace for their wedding anniversary.

In fact, he recognized that there was an occasional crusty staff member who obviously did not like there job. But focusing on all the positive staff members blocked out the negative thoughts and filled his mind with things about the home that he was grateful and thankful for.

At this time, instead of focusing on the fact that Ann had to wait till her roommate was bathed before she received attention, he focused on the fact that Ann was kept clean had proper skin care and overall received good nursing care. She had no skin breakdown while in the nursing home for seven years. He focused on the specialized equipment they had to transfer Ann from the bed to a chair with relative ease. He began to fill his mind with positive thoughts about the home bringing him peace of mind. All the negative things about the home seemed minimal when he started focusing on all the positive aspects.

In any event, in his prolonged grief Jack suffered terribly from loneliness. He missed the warm loving relationship he once had with Ann. He missed sleeping next to her warm soft body. He missed the intimacy they both shared. He missed her wonderful home cooked meals. He missed going on all the cruises they enjoyed so much and other travels they went on. The fun, laughter, hugs, kisses and just being together was so painfully missed. He could not pull himself out of his grief. He grieved for his wife for over seven years ever since she had her tragic stroke.

In due time, he decided instead of being obsessed with the things he missed he would fill his time with activities that brought him joy. He found his true passion and became a prolific song and poem writer. He made plans to meet with a woman who was a professional singer to see if she could help him put the songs he wrote to music. He started working with a friend to write a book and passed his time reading books and listening to music. He wrote many poems too and started sketching art pieces. He was so happy that he found his true passion that brought joy into his life.

In the meantime, he was asking each day who can I encourage, who can I cheer up, who can I help, who can I bless today? His loneliness was being overcome slowly by giving to others.

Once, Jack began to read with diligence Joel Osteen's book ***The Power Of I Am,*** the huge challenge of getting out and interacting with others was becoming much easier to accomplish. The door began to open, and he started giving himself permission to participate in his life again. All the emotional chains were slowly coming off being replaced by positive thinking. He began to see himself as great and began seeing his exceptional self. He gained the insight that the solution is from within not outside of him, and that he must realize and believe that he is awesome. He acquired insight that he had to change his **I Am's**, and that he had everything he needed within himself to make the dramatic change.

Now, he looked in the mirror and said I am talented, I am smart, I am strong, I am disciplined I'm focused and I'm awesome. Instead of saying I've been dealt a bad deal, I'm not smart, I'm sad I'm lonely, I lost my life, my life is worthless, I've lost my life's savings.

Once he realized that words create one's reality, he was able to embrace the positive words more readily. He saw that words are powerful**,** and the **I AM's** are influential. He realized if he had to fulfill his destiny, he had to shake those negatives voices and had to stop inviting weakness. He rose above the forces that made him feel intimidated, inferior, unqualified, insecure, unconfident, and uninteresting.

Thus, focusing on positive **I AM's** he was able to develop an appreciation his strengths and talents, and he developed his spiritual muscles of strength, endurance, and confidence. This newfound self-confidence enabled him to meet old friends that he once felt he didn't fit in with and began interacting with them on a regular basis. He met with Coach Polo frequently and enjoyed talking sports, politics, and family matters. He interacted with his friend Mary on an ongoing basis and felt enhanced energy after each interaction. He met with old friends in a local diner to have breakfast. His self-confidence allowed him to meet new friends with ease and found the loneliness diminishing dramatically.

Next, another huge challenge for Jack was dealing with the anxiety of the system. He defined the system as all those governmental agencies he had to deal with after Ann's stroke. The system included social services, IRS, and social security. Social Services was a bureaucratic nightmare for Jack. Filling out all the paperwork and recertifying Ann's services every year was a task far beyond his capability. He was low on energy due to his grief and his thinking was not clear.

Additionally, he had to deal with an ill-natured, cankerous, crockety, condescending lady at the social service office who was void of any empathy. She obviously did not like her job and never went the extra mile to help Jack.

Furthermore, he had to take money out of the IRA to pay the nursing home for Ann's nursing care. This created a tax liability that each year was difficult for Jack to pay each year. To make matters worse his bank closed, and he had to find a new bank. Getting his and Ann's social security direct payment deposits took forever to accomplish due to the social security departments delayed lack luster response. This left Jack in a bind, because now there was no money in the checking to pay his monthly bills. He couldn't sleep at night worrying about all this bureaucratic red tape disaster.

Surprisingly, after reading Joel Osteen's book **The Power Of I AM**, he began to say I can do this. I'm smart, I'm strong. I'm disciplined. He recognized his limitations in dealing with this mess, but was determined to do it. He wisely sought out resources to help him.

Specifically, a friend of his helped him set up all the accounts in the new bank. He asked his accountant to help him to fill out the recertification paperwork with social services. His accountant took care of the IRA paperwork.

Moreover, his son helped to bail him out until all the payments from his pension and social security took place properly so he could pay his bills.

Now, he asked the new bank to help him get the social security payments deposited since his attempts to call social security failed. Social security could not set an appointment for Jack to go in person for at least three months and meanwhile the checks would have been going to the bank that closed. His new bank was helpful to Jack. They faxed in the request for the change since Jack couldn't get an appointment with social security for three months. He saw that by asking for help he could get these difficult tasks accomplished giving him peace of mind.

Lastly, he was determined not to let the social service lady's crusty attitude get him down. He had faith in his ability to work with her and not let her poor attitude get in the way of accomplishing his mission.

Finally, his renewed attitude changed his thinking from I **can't** do all this, to I **can do** this, and **I will** by asking for help. He now feels more peace of mind in this area and is sleeping better now. It was a load taken off his mind and back.

Moreover, the book ***Think Better, Live Better*** enabled Jack to learn how to clear out all the negative things people have said about him. He realized that he couldn't stop people such as his brothers from saying negative things, but he can choose whether he will dwell on them or not.

In short, Jack became aware that the only power that a label had over him was the power he gave to it. He was no longer shaken by the things his brothers have spoken to him and his family. The mean comments that were contaminating his mind, and that he was feeding and watering have now been reprogramed in his thought process so that no strongholds in his mind would hold him back. Once Jack understood why his brothers acted the way they did, he was able to hit the delete button and step into freedom.

Markedly, the relationship with his brothers was a grueling hurdle for Jack to overcome. He over time came to the realization that his one brother displayed narcissism, and bullying behavior probably stemming from the abusive household he was also raised in.

In fact, that one brother patterned his behavior after his dad's behavior. His brother was not going to change, and Jack knew to protect his family he had to cut the toxic relationship. He made a conscious decision however not to talk bad about his brother to his sisters, his other brother or people in the community when asked how his brother Jimmy was doing. He thought that would add fuel to the fire and keep him focused on negative thoughts. Finally, not dealing with his brother's drama at holidays, birthdays, and other events, brought him peace of mind for himself and his family. He consciously decided not to harp on all the negative things his brother said to his wife and son and Jack himself.

Successfully, he was able to eliminate all the memories of how his brother hurt him and his family making room for only positive thoughts. When his brother's unpleasant thoughts surrounding his mom's death and other hurtful interactions came knocking on the door to his mind, he put a no vacancy sign on the door eliminating them completely.

Indeed, he saw clearly that he had to remove the bad soil filled with weeds and rocks, so his seeds of joy, happiness, enthusiasm and vibrance could bloom and thrive. He had no choice, but to discontinue his association with his brother for the sake of Jack's family. This brought tremendous peace to his mind to Jack.

Another key point, Jack's financial situation was very bleak. This was an enormous concern for Jack. Since his life's savings went to the home for Ann's nursing care he had to survive on a small pension and social security. He worried whether he'd have enough money to pay the monthly bills and pay the taxes each year incurred by the IRA withdrawal for Ann's care.

In the foreground, he was very frugal trying to save money for gas, bills and taxes. He ate mostly sardines and spam from the dollar store, hamburgers from McDonald's and Kentucky fried chicken. He wore clothes he bought over 15 years ago. He had no TV, no internet service, no CD Player, or credit cards and discontinued his Sirius radio subscription. He had no need for materialistic items. At age 77 he still cut his own grass, he washes his clothes at the local laundromat and gets a cheap haircut at the nursing home.

Specifically, the only thing he had was his radio with the basic stations to listen to such as the news, and the sports programs that he liked, and a cell phone so he could text his sisters, son and communicate with the home in case of an emergency. His son bought him a DVD player to watch movies that gave him some joy. He finally broke down and bought an inexpensive CD player so he could listen to his favorite tunes. Since he grew up with nothing, always kept out of debt and always payed everything with cash, saving money was no problem for him. It's just that there was not that much to save.

In the center of this, he renewed his faith in God, he felt the tide of this battle will turn around. Each night he declared God's favor. He announced that today I will come out of financial strife. I will come into increase overflow and abundance and refused to live negative, worried, anxious, and stressed out.

In fact, when he put his faith in God suddenly his son called him gave him reassurance that he would help if he ran into a shortage one particular month due to some unexpected expense like car problems or appliance issues. This unexpected call gave him immense peace of mind. He put his trust in God that all would work out and that allowed him to put his worries aside.

Quickly, many light bulbs went on as Jack read the book ***Your Best Life Now.*** Jack learned for his emotional and physical health, he had to let go of all the bitterness he was feeling surrounding the anger over the loss of his life's savings. This was a huge source of his bitterness that was extremely arduous for Jack to overcome. He was angered by the fact that he was owned by the nursing home and that nest egg they put away for retirement was being obliterated and could not be used for anything but Ann's nursing care. He knew if he continued to fixate on this loss and harbor this bitterness in his heart it would prevent him from ever being genuinely happy.

Markedly, he took what God has given him and made the most out of it by trying to see some positive aspect of this extraordinary loss. He began to refocus his thinking and tried to see that if he didn't have that nest egg to provide nursing care for Ann, she may be placed in one of those Medicaid homes where the care was subpar. He felt comfort in knowing at least that she was not in a home that let patients lie in their own feces for long periods of time. And a home where patients were not fed properly. A home that was not clean and one that had rodents running around. A home so short staffed that patients were not turned in bed often enough to prevent bed sores. With these thoughts he was able to accept better the loss of his life's savings.

Prior to reading Joel Osteen's books the anger and negative thinking of being dealt a bad deal plagued Jack's mind and he questioned why God did this to him and Ann. He was angry at God. He blamed God for Ann's stroke. Holding on to feelings of bitterness and resentment was poisoning his future.

Thus, Osteen's insights let him see if he allowed himself to remain bitter and resentful and continued to blame God for this tragedy his life would be filled with thoughts of self-pity, feeling sorry for himself, thinking always that life didn't deal him a fair hand.

To be sure, he became cognitively aware that this mind set would poison and contaminate his remaining years. It was time to allow the emotional wounds to heal and to let go of the excuses for feeling sorry for himself. He comprehended well that God never promised life would be fair and thinking of what could have been, what should have been, what might have been, was preventing him from taking back his life. He quit asking why this? Why that? Why me?

Amazingly, after reading the Joel Osteen books, he was able to walk out on the emotional bondage in which he was living. He knew nobody could do that but himself. He released all the pains, and hurts. He left the past behind and didn't question God and stayed in an attitude of faith. He was tired of drifting through life taking whatever comes his way. He took action to rise above his obstacles by staying positive, thanking God for his blessings, believing his life would be turned around so that he could experience joy, happiness, and peace once again. And over time his joy and peace were restored.

# 6

# Bringing Joy, Happiness and Peace Back to the Heart

**Finally, Jack removed** most of the chains that had shackled him for years and came out of the cave to see a new realty and vision. He renewed fully his faith in God. When he realized the key to living a liberating life was to turn the unfair things that have happened over to God. God is fighting his battles. He walked with new confidence with pep in his step, a smile on his face and a song in his heart. He believed God knows what he needs, and God will bring new energies into his life. This change in attitude left the door wide open for God to right all the wrongs that took place in Jack' life.

Specifically, he took all those disappointments, setbacks, and losses that shook his faith to the foundation and let go of all the hurts, pain, and losses. He rose up and said "I don't care how hard this is, I'm not going to let this get the best of me. I'm moving on with my life".

Adamantly, he refused to let the enemy deceive him into indulging in self-pity, fretting, feeling sorry for himself, or having a chip on his shoulder. He stopped asking questions why me, why didn't things work out in my life, and why did Ann and I get this bum deal dealt to us? He quit wasting his time on trying to figure out something that he couldn't change.

To point out Joel Osteen says you can't unscramble eggs. What's done is done. So, Jack shook himself out of the doldrums. He quit mourning over his loses and started to receive Gods mercy and love feeling confident God had another plan for him. He believed and trusted in God for a better future. A future that rejected bitterness to fester inside that would poison his future.

He quit living in a negative frame of mind stewing about something that took place in the past. He started focusing on what he could change rather than what he could not change. He knew if God closed one door another door would open revealing something bigger and better. He let go of the past and started living each day with faith and expectancy.

Finally, he was able to say God I'm putting these issues in your hands. I've done everything I know to do. I'm not going to be trapped in the past. I'm going to move on with my life knowing You are in control. God did take his most horrendous battlefield and turned it into a great blessing field.

Thus, his life was revitalized. He focused on getting his songs that he wrote composed to music, he considered writing a book to help others, he wrote poems in a prolific manner, he sketched some art work, he was getting out, having lunch and breakfast with others periodically, and visiting friends to talk about sports and in particular his beloved Yankees.

Explicitly, the feeling of not fitting in with others dissipated as he discovered now that he had so much to offer in wisdom and helpful hints. He sought out resources to deal with the complicated paperwork required by the system easing his mind that all was done properly. He had renewed energy and vibrance when visiting his wife that was refreshing for her. And, presently he has more to offer her in making his visits more interesting and exciting for Ann. Now that his spirit was healed, he was able to help Ann heal her broken spirit.

To be sure, it was extraordinary how Jack got his life back by renewing his faith in God and reading Joel Osteen's books. Jack is an amazing person. One to be admired for all his hard work in turning his victim mentality into a victorious life with abundance, joy and fulfillment.

Thus, releasing all those chains allowed Jack to focus on his lovely wife, so he can help her re-engineer her mind to minimize the bad moods. He's wearing a whole new demeanor proudly and feeling as good as he did in high school when he was a star athlete playing sports. He felt back then he was invincible, indestructible, and unshakeable and always forged forward with a never give up attitude, and that's how he feels now. He feels so great knowing he's in charge and that he has a quality life.

Finally, all the emotional chains were released, and Jack was free of bondage and learned how to nourish the seeds of joy, happiness, and peace of mind. His renewed faith in God enabled him to bring quality back to his life and leave his former life of defeat, anger, insecurity, low self-esteem, and bitterness. He now thinks big, has a vision.

At the present time, he knows now he has the self-confidence and self-esteem to help others. That gives him a sense of joy and fulfillment. He woke up every morning making a choice to be happy and to have a good day. He looked forward to being a blessing to others through his smile, advice, helping hand, and whatever he felt God was directing him to do.

# 7

# Unleashed Emotional Chains

**The emotional chains** that Jack was successful in unleashing are summarized below. As he unlocked these chains, he brought joy, happiness, and vibrancy back into his life.

**Loneliness** Jack overcame his loneliness by focusing on putting a song that he wrote to music. He connected more often with his former coach each time the Yankees played baseball. He continued to read books and listen to the *Oldies but Goodies Music* that he enjoyed so much. This music brought back positive memories of high school. He continued to interact by phone and text with his sisters and his friends. He was filling up his time with activities that brought him joy. He was asking each day who can I encourage, who can I cheer up, who can I help, who can I bless today?

He resigned himself to the fact that he would no longer enjoy the close intimacy and share a warm bed with his wife anymore. He was so faithful to his wife that seeing another woman would never even pass his mind. But he no longer lingered over his loses and refocused on making his visits in the nursing home with his wife as pleasant as possible.

**Guilt Internalized by Ann's Bad Moods** Jack now understands more fully why Ann lashed out at him and has learned to remain calm and peaceful during the burst of insults. He has mastered how to manage her outbursts and they no longer leave him feeling guilty or hurt. He keeps his mind free of negative thoughts and will only let positive ones enter his mind and heart.

**Frustration and Anger of the Nursing Home** Jack concentrated on all the positive things about the home. To his surprise there were so many positive aspects to the nursing home as he viewed them and moved away from spotlighting the few negative things. He had peace of mind knowing that the home had full array of specialty medical services available should an emergency pop up in the middle of the night. The nursing care was good, they had a wonderful activities department to keep the residents involved with such as holiday, birthday and anniversary celebrations, youth volunteers, support dog visits, occupational activities, creative arts and so much more. Additionally, they had an active physical therapy department and psychological counseling. The nursing home was clean and well maintained. It was reassuring and comforting to know the nursing home had outstanding state inspection reports. He emphasized these positive aspects of the nursing home instead of brooding over an occasional crusty staff member and the lack of gourmet cruise type food.

**Anxiety Created by The System: Social Services, IRS, Social Security**
It must be remembered that in the past filling out all the paperwork for these three agencies was overwhelming and a source of constant anxiety. However, Jack now sought out help with all the complex paperwork required by all these agencies instead of trying to figure it out himself. He became more comfortable asking for help from others. This help gave him peace of mind and took the burden off his shoulders. As the paperwork was completed, he put it in Gods hand and told himself it will all work out.

**Getting Out with Others** After reading Joel Osteen's book the power of I Am Jack no longer felt uncomfortable with others. The feeling of not fitting in has dissipated and when the opportunity presented itself, he joined others in various activities. All the emotional chains that led the fundamental problem of low self-esteem started coming off and his thinking of not seeing himself highly was being replaced by positive thinking. He began to see himself as great and began seeing his own amazingness and felt more comfortable fitting in with others. He learned that stories he told to others were enjoyed and received well by others.

**Fear with Financial Situation** Jack grew up with nothing and living frugal was never a problem for him. His only concern was if he had an emergency with a needed car or appliance repair would he have enough money to take care of it. This created fear in Jack' mind. He always took pride in paying his bills on time but worried that there may be a time where he might be late in a monthly payment. When Jack put all his financial woes in the hands of God things turned around for him. His son stepped up to the plate and told him never to worry. When and if you ever run short on a month's bill, I'll be there to cover it. This gave Jack great peace of mind. As he renewed his faith in God and no longer let his financial status keep him awake at night anymore.

**Anger-Loss of Life Savings** he was not tempted anymore to sit around and mourn over the loss of his life's savings. He stopped thinking of what he lost and stopped obsessing with how unfair his situation was, and how his life will never be the same. He did not allow himself to wave the white flag of surrender. He accentuated positive thinking and said to himself I'm coming out of this thing, I'm going to be OK, and with God's help I'll embrace God's can-do power. He became grateful that the money was there to provide Ann with nursing care in a home that had a good reputation and an excellent state investigation rating. He shudders to think where Ann would have been placed if the money were not there.

**Bitterness of Being Dealt a Bad Deal.** Jack learned that the challenge of his wife's stroke in his life knocked him down on the outside, but the key to living in victory is to learn how to get up on the inside. He was knocked down outside his control, but learned to stand up high inside. He developed a victor mentality and his attitude was, this bad deal is not going to defeat me. This misfortune is not going to steal my joy. I am not going to dawdle in a victim mentality. He was able to stop thinking about this tragedy and stayed excited to his other blessings that God has given him.

**Dysfunctional Relationship with Brothers** He came to terms with his brothers' negative attitude and made a decision that at his age with little time left he had to surround himself with positive people who enhanced his energy rather that those that drain his energy. He stopped thinking of all the memories and hurtful comments his brothers made about his wife and son. The decision to cut off the toxic ties with his brothers gave him peace of mind.

**The Hurtful Experiences Endured by his Father's Abuse** Jack continued to disconfirm all the negative labels his father put in his mind that made Jack feel like he would never amount to much, that he was a bum, not talented, that he was not smart, that he was a loser. He removed all the feelings of inferiority, anxiety, intimidation, fear, unworthiness and guilt out of his mind. He was no longer going to let his father haunt him anymore. He decided to let his past make him better not bitter.

**Living in the Car Like a Hermit** This one issue is still a work in progress not accomplished completely yet. His wife has told him not to throw anything away and so he's been held hostage to the guilt she lays on him about not throwing stuff away. To overcome his guilt, he's reading a book on how to declutter one's home. The book has given him some insight as to why he is unable to get rid of the clutter is his home.

After reading the book he has made major strides in de-cluttering his home. He has a dumpster to put the clutter in. He's talks about a yard sale and plans to donate some items such as the medical equipment to those who need the equipment. He is slowly but surely getting other items in the dumpster.

He is reframing his thoughts now to delete the guilt about making his home comfortable for him so he can once again live in his house. He has at least come to the realization that he no longer wants to be held hostage to the stuff that he no longer uses, no longer works, and no longer gives him joy. Although he has made strides in this area, he still has a long way to go in this area. Despite offers from his sister Ellen and son to help him de clutter his house he still has not accepted their help. This is the only chain not fully unleashed.

Amazingly, he adjusted his thoughts and filled his mind with the positive labels that his basketball coach put on him. This helped him overcome his prolonged grief. Coach Polo labels flowed through his mind. He heard them whisper in his ear you are bright, talented, strong, athletic, hardworking, victorious, and respectful. With the mentoring from Coach Polo Jack was able to let go of his past childhood trauma brought on by his abusive alcoholic father and now was making significant progress in overcoming his prolonged grief brought on by his wife's stroke.

Meanwhile, all these emotional chains that Jack removed made Mary delighted. She was so pleased with Jack' progress in taking back his life and living life now with enthusiasm filled with joy, happiness and peace of mind. He was a new person. He has purpose in life, feels his life is worthwhile and is looking forward to fulfilling his destiny. He can feel joy and happiness once again.

Markedly, he has come out of the cave almost completely once and for all except for decluttering his home. He is crossing the finish line standing high inside, proud of himself and recognizing what an amazing person he is.

Notably, Jack was knocked down many times in his life but he made up his mind he was not going to stay down, he was determined to live in victory and determined to work out the multiple problems that kept popping up in his life. Jack had a remarkable transformation and now looks forward to what the future will bring.

Expressly, in commemoration of Jack' significant achievements in releasing the emotional chains that shackled his life in misery, Mary wrote this second poem for Jack entitled, *An Ode To Jack*.

## Ode to Jack

*You bring joy to you heart*
*You bring humor to your soul*
*Your jokes make others laugh out of control*
*You lifted your spirits to the sky*
*Talking with you my friend*
*Is a natural high*
*You created a new life for yourself*
*With fulfillment, what a tribute to thyself*

*A life with purpose and joy*
*A life filled with happiness you can now enjoy*
*You came out of the cave*
*With courage standing brave*
*Your life is an inspiration to all*
*On how to live with abundance and stand tall*

*You changed your mindset from defeat to victory*
*From weakness to vibrancy*
*You've taken back your life*
*While still supporting your beloved wife*
*God was good to you*
*Because you believed*
*From his strength you drew*
*So now you no longer grieved*
*Never give up is your motto*
*You tore those chains off*
*So, no more grief would follow*
*You worked hard to achieve this payoff*
*No more anger, fear, guilt, or bitterness,*
*No more meaningless*

*No more insecurity, depression, or anxiety*
*On to vibrancy, energy, and generosity*

*On to joyfulness, peace, happiness*
*On to fullness, faith, and freshness*
*Looking for who to help, who to cheer up,*
*Looking for who to help standup*
*Looking for who to encourage and bless today*
*You thanked the Lord, for blessings received each day*

## The Flower Button

Mary read a book entitled *FWE Lohmann: Elizabeth Van Lew's Civil War Spy* by Virginia Lohmann Nodhturft. One section in the book Mary found very touching. In the Civil War days, the woman cut off their bronze flower button from their dress or coat and they gave it to their husbands to put in their trousers for comfort when things got bad and they were feeling low in spirits. The flower button gave their husbands a feeling of comfort. Angela Lohmann gave her bronze button to her husband when he was in the Battle of Bull Run before, he became a Union spy. When he became a spy, he was transporting a family of black slaves across the border to safety and got caught. He was thrown in the worst prison in Richmond Virginia. Angela asked Miss Van Lew the woman who headed the large spy ring in Richmond, Virginia to smuggle the flower button into the prison for FWE. Miss Van Lew bribed one of the prison guards and he brought the flower button into the prison to comfort FWE while he was being tortured for the names of the other spies.

FWE wrote the following poem about the flower button:

## The Flower Button

*Holding my love's flower button helps me fight*
*It gives me strength to get through the night*
*It gives me comfort for sure*
*For during the torture, I can endure*
*As I hold this flower button close and near*
*It lifts my sprit to overcome my fear*
*As I lie here awake at night*
*I wonder what's in store for me come daylight*
*As I look at the flower button, I count the blessings bestowed on me*
*My dear Angela and boys who sat on my knee*
*With flower button in hand I look up to Thee*
*It's clear the blessings I see*
*I need to shake off my feeling of defeat*
*So, my sprit will not retreat*
*Please Dear Lord turn my spirit from sour to sweet*
*So, my purpose can be fulfilled and complete*
*With your help, I will not let my spirit be crushed or die*
*For my positive thoughts are my biggest ally*
*Please Dear Lord let positive thoughts flood my mind*
*So, my energies will not be undermined*
*I pray I will look back someday and see where I've been*
*So, I can help others to never give in*
*Success in facing adversity lies in feeding your life with positive thoughts*
*Thoughts of sunsets, trees, flowers, music, water, gratefulness or other "ought"*
*Looking for ways to be a blessing to others*
*Will allow me to sleep tight under the covers.*
*Thank you, dear flower button, for helping me stay strong*
*And thank you Dear Lord for enforcing my faith*
*You guided me to see the sense of right and wrong*
*Your belief in me kept me safe*

With this in mind, Mary got the idea from this book to give Jack a white flower button that came from her white dress that she wore on the evening of her retirement party. She cut the white flower button off and gave it to Jack to put on his bookshelf or dresser. She told him to hold it in times of low spirits to give him comfort on that particular day. Holding the flower button would let him know she was thinking of him and that he had the strength to get through whatever was weighing heavy on his heart. Jack was touched by the gesture and was very appreciative of the kind thought.

## Song Dedication

Mary dedicated the song I Hope You Dance by Lee Ann Womack to Jack.

### I Hope You Dance
*Lee Ann Womack*

I hope you never lose your sense of wonder
You get your fill to eat but always keep that hunger
May you never take one single breath for granted
God forbid love ever leave you empty handed
I hope you still feel small when you stand beside the ocean
Whenever one door closes I hope one more opens
Promise me that you'll give fate the fighting chance
And when you get the choice to sit it out or dance
I hope you dance
I hope you dance

I hope you never fear those mountains in the distance
Never settle for the path of least resistance
Living might mean taking chances but they're worth taking
Lovin' might be a mistake but it's worth making
Don't let some hell bent heart leave you bitter
When you come close to selling out reconsider
Give the heavens above more than just a passing glance
And when you get the choice to sit it out or dance
I hope you dance
(Time is a wheel in constant motion always)
I hope you dance
(Rolling us along)
I hope you dance
(Tell me who wants to look back on their years and wonder)
I hope you dance
(Where those years have gone)

*I hope you still feel small when you stand by the ocean*
*Whenever one door closes, I hope one more opens*
*Promise me that you'll give faith the fighting chance*
*And when you get the choice to sit it out or dance*
*Dance*
*I hope you dance*
*I hope you dance*
*(Time is a wheel in constant motion always)*
*I hope you dance*
*(Rolling us along)*
*I hope you dance*
*(Tell me who wants to look back on their years and wonder)*
*I hope you dance*
*(Where those years have gone)*
*(Tell me who wants to look back on their years and wonder)*
*I hope you dance*
*(Where those years have gone)*

Printed with written permission of Marc D. Sanders
Songwriters: Tia Sillers, & Mark Sanders.

## Humpty Dumpty

Broken Humpty Dumpy was put back together. Mary was overjoyed that Jack made such phenomenal progress in taking back his life that is now filled with joy and happiness. He dreams big, he prays big and expects good things to happen each day. He has a wonderful feeling of being in control of his life knowing the decisions and choices he makes determine the quality of his life.

Specifically, he chose to think of others, put his faith in God, and do good for others and thus was his answer to a happy life. He is flying high like an eagle experiencing peace and freedom for the first time in over eight years. He's flying over the pecking crows and is determined to keep his mind filled with positive thinking and letting go of all the negative past.

Truly, it was astonishing how Jack was able to refocus his mind and transform his life. He enlarged his vision, developed a healthy self-image was able to let go of the past and move on to fulfilling destiny that was to become a blessing to others.

Indeed, Jack found giving all he had to others in terms of smiles, positive comments, advice, a listening ear, encouragement, and support was so rewarding for him. It fostered his ability to choose on a daily basis to be happy. He moved away from thinking of himself and paying attention to all his problems. He thought in terms of others looking for opportunities to be a blessing to others whether it was a kind word, a smile, just listening, a hug, providing advice, or helping in some other way.

Markedly, his passion and zest for life returned with fire in his heart. He was excited about his dreams and his future. *Romans 12:12* reminded Jack that he can choose to live his life with enthusiasm. The scripture says, "Never lag in zeal, but aglow and on fire, serving the lord enthusiastically". This describes Jack' new life. *Aglow* with God's presence, on fire with enthusiasm.

Thus, he learned to keep his heart open to compassion and being in tune to what God wanted him to do. And Jack will never sit out, he will always dance. As Jack renewed his faith in God, he particularly liked Psalm 16:11 You make known to me the path of life; in your presence there is fullness of joy; at your right hand are pleasures forever.

Specifically, this psalm gave Jack inspiration that his renewed relationship with God will direct his steps in his path of life and trusting in God will bring joy and other pleasures of happiness, abundance and prosperity so he can be a blessing to others in need. He knew that God would present him with new opportunities that will thrust him into a new level of his destiny.

Indeed, Jack is like the palm tree that Joel Osteen talked about in *Psalm 92:11* the righteous will flourish like a palm tree. Joel visited a community after a hurricane one time and houses were destroyed, big oak trees were uprooted, but the palm trees still were standing.

Frequently, during a severe storm the palm tree bends way over flattened on the ground looking as though its life is gone forever. When the storm is over the palm tree bounces back in place stronger than it was before the storm. No storm could destroy the palm tree. It was in a temporary state of defeat, but after the storm it rose up high in victory.

Unlike the oak tree that looked stronger on the outside than the palm tree. During the severe storm, the oak tree cracked and uprooted and lied on the ground in defeat never to rise up again. It was defeated and did not have the ability to spring back to victory like the palm tree. Jack walked through the struggles in life like the palm tree. This is how God made Jack. When the storms hit, Jack was able to withstand them, even the most difficult storms.

In short, *Psalm129* says: *"From my earliest youth my enemies have persecuted me, but they have never been able to finish me off."* This Psalm sums up Jack' life.

Particularly, depression couldn't finish Jack off, loss of life savings couldn't finish Jack off, the critics at the nursing home couldn't finish Jack off, loneliness couldn't finish Jack off, loss of intimacy with his wife, didn't finish Jack off, negative family interactions didn't finish Jack, his father's negative words and actions didn't finish him off. He got knocked down, but he got up again, he had setbacks, but he still in the game, he went through loss, but he deleted his bitterness he kept moving forward, none of these setbacks could finish him off. He was a fighter and stuck to his motto **never give up** that he learned and embraced from Coach Polo and was reinforced by Joel Osteen.

In fact, Jack felt many times that his life had caved in on top of himself knocking him off his feet and pushing him down. But he had a victor's attitude and mentality and stayed in an attitude of faith. He did not let himself lapse into his former negative thinking, complaining, or blaming God. He said I may not understand all this adversity, but he knew God was in control. He believed all things would work together for his good. He had faith that God would turn around all the suffering and use it to his advantage.

Expressly, he thanked God for bringing him through all the adversity and knew no matter what he faced in life he knew how to get up inside. Nothing was going to keep Jack down. He took comfort in Psalm 46 *"God is present to help in times of need"*. During his difficulties he heard God whispering "Jack I'm in control. It's going to work out, I have you in the palm of My hand". It was finishing grace pushing him forward moving him to his destiny. He felt at peace, strength, and resolve.

In summary, in Jack's life he lived, he loved, he cried, he hurt he's made mistakes, but most of all he learned. We don't know how Jack's life will end, but we know one thing you will never see in any of his texts, thoughts or conversations with words that say: I Gave Up! You will see words that say, "Never Give Up"! Never give up, keep standing, keep praying, keep believing and keep hoping in faith.

*8*

# POEMS DEPICTING HOW JACK FELT IN AND OUT OF THE CAVE

**THE SKETCH BELOW** depicts Jack's miserable state of mind in the cave with chains of lonliness, anger, guilt, shame, unworthiness, fear and anxiety that shachled him for years while imprisoned in Plato's Cave. And it shows how he feels when resuurected from the cave. He's happy and smiling with the chains broken off as he escapes and feels like a free person again. He has a fresh new vison for his life and is filled with energy and vibrancy.

**Sketch By: Pete Delmonico**

The following poems were written by Pete Delmonico to portray how miserable and lonely Jack felt in the cave and how refreshed and vibrant he felt when he was resurrected from the cave.

# Escape the Cave

*Living in a Plato Cave is not what you should do*
*It's dark and very lonely it's like a prison yes, it's true*

*To end up in a life with no value*
*And no one to look up to*
*You have let yourself down and given up the dream of being true to you*
*So, the cave is a haven that shields you from the true view*

*To step outside is awesome a learning curve to you*
*Further out you wander you'll find the real you*
*It takes a bit of nerve to pull it off its true*
*But if you have a bit of nerve it's beneficial to you*
*And a trusted friend can help you cause the sunlight it may blind*
*But not forever, for you'll soon see in your mind*

*The reward of leaving Plato's Cave behind*
*So, in the end it's worth it to yourself be kind*
*And go on and find yourself that you foolishly left behind*
*Author: Pete Delmonico*

# **Rescued from the Cave**

*There's a man in a cave what should he do if he's to survive*
*He must come out yes that's no lie*
*But he doesn't know how even though he tries*

*Along come a person, a person out of the blue*
*Compassionate person he once knew*

*Helped him to escape out of the cave before it was too late*
*All of a sudden to his surprise the sunlight hit him in both of his eyes,*
*it was his fate*

*He finally saw the light of day*
*What he missed he couldn't say he just knew it was great to break away*

*So, forward he goes and thanks to a friend*
*Someone who cared to make him whole again*

*So, it's his glorious day*
*He's out in the sunlight and hopes everyday*
*That his friend will continue to be a mainstay*

*Author: Pete Delmonico*

## Reaching My Destiny

*I was a cave man, so it was true*
*Then God helped me by sending me you*
*You told me to not be afraid to see*
*The sunlight outside forever free*
*So, it is something now I can see*
*The cave I went to forever to be*
*Then I was rescued, you came to me*
*God gave me you to break me free*
*You took my hand and helped me*
*To be out in the open society*
*You helped me be a believer in God and find my destiny*
*And the need to let my mind open so I could be free*
*Free the shackles and cave mentality*
*A brand-new mindset you gave to me*
*So, you made me listen what God has for me*
*And I'll always be searching for my passion to reach my destiny*
*Author: Pete Delmonico*

## **Resurrected from the Cave**

*I didn't know how to do it*
*But you helped me get through it*

*To leave the past and misery behind*
*So, I could release all the painful grind*
*I could not see the future*
*I was such a lonely miserable creature*

*And never saw that I was blind*
*Being stuck in the cave that's in your mind*
*Gets to feel normal over time*

*But when released to the outside you can see*
*Wasn't worthwhile and it stifles your personality*
*You came near to me to help me get free*
*You helped me see the cave that enslaved me*

*So now I don't have to wonder why*
*You came to lead and teach me how to come alive*

*I now understand how I got stuck and must say goodbye*
*I'm so very thankful to the person that is you*
*Who took the time to recue me*
*I value your true view, I no longer feel like a cave abductee*

*No more self-pity for me*
*I'm always grateful to thee*
*For bringing you to me*
*No more chains to shackle me*
*Cause I am an escapee from the awful cave in me*
*Author: Pete Delmonico*

## No More Cave for Me

*The cave is empty now it's missing me you see*
*I rose above the loss and pain it's no place to be*
*Chained in the cave made me miss the life I need*
*And possibilities and opportunities abundant in society*

*The caves is dark and gloomy it's not a place to be*
*It's heartache hotel in your mind for many folks like me*
*It hides your shame and lonely life until you're set free*
*I never knew how bad is was until you came to me*

***The cave is empty now it's missing me you see***
***I rose above the loss and pain it's no place to be***
***Chained in the cave made me miss the life I need***
***And possibilities and opportunities abundant in society***

*It only takes a helping hand for one to be set free*
*If you enter the cave mentality and suffer in misery*
*Then get the help you need to set yourself free*
*It only takes a helping hand for one to be set free*

***The cave is empty now its missing me you see***
***I rose above the loss and pain it's no place to be***
***Chained in the cave made me miss the life I need***
***With possibilities and opportunities abundant in society***

*It only takes a little help for someone who can see*
*To drag you out of there so you can really be*
*God gave me the greatest gift of bringing you to me*
*To help me find reality*

***The cave is empty now its missing me you see***
***I rose above the loss and pain it's no place to be***

*Chained in the cave made me miss the life I need*
*With possibilities and opportunities abundant in society*

*I found the fragrance in the breeze*
*The sunlight through the trees*
*I found the smell of strawberries in the field*
*The sights and smells so pleasing were revealed*

**The cave is empty now its missing me you see**
**I rose above the loss and pain it's no place to be**
**Chained in the cave made me miss the life I need**
**With possibilities and opportunities abundant in society**

*The sound of singing birds was music to my ears*
*I was venturing out on new frontiers*
*Feeling the wind flow through my hair*
*I no longer felt the pain and despair*

**The cave is empty now its missing me you see**
**I rose above the loss and pain it's no place to be**
**Chained in the cave made me miss the life I need**
**With possibilities and opportunities abundant in society**

*To leave the cave behind and find a place for me*
*And feel a desperate need to reach my destiny*
*I now feel joy and happiness*
*And no longer will settle for less*

**The cave is empty now its missing me you see**
**I rose above the loss and pain it's no place to be**
**Chained in the cave made me miss the life I need**
**With possibilities and opportunities abundant in society**

*Authors: Pete Delmonico & Ginny Nodhturft*

Pete and Ginny transformed Pete's poem ***No More Cave for Me*** into a song that describes how awful it was for Jack to live isolated in Plato's cave in misery wallowing in resentment, bitterness, anger, anxiety, self-pity, loneliness, and guilt. It describes how he led a life that lacked energy, vibrancy, and spirituality. He was defeated in his mind and was not able to overcome the barriers trapped in his thoughts.

Further, the song explains that it took a friend and a renewal of faith to develop the courage to escape the cave to see a new vison. Once resurrected from the cave a new life was waiting where he found his passion and purpose in life. A life filled with joy and happiness. And the cave is now empty.

# 9

# THE MIGHTY HERO BECOMES A MIRACLE

**NOW THAT JACK** has taken back his life and is living a life of joy, happiness and peace his destiny in life has now focused on helping his wife Ann. He wanted to renew her faith in God, and to restore her soul and spirit so she too can lead the remaining years in peace. He knew that words have creative power. He realized that when he spoke, he give life to what he was saying. He wanted to instill hope, and encourage big dreams for Ann. He wanted her to declare favor over her life and her future.

This was going to be a monumental task because Ann was in a state of grief over all her losses. She had a defeated mentality and was immersed in self-pity. She verbalized over and over like a broken record, why did this happen to me, what did I do to deserve this, why has God punished me, it's not fair, I was given a raw deal, why? She begged Jack to take her home. She lost her enthusiasm for life and wanted to die. She continued to say I've seen my best days, it's all downhill from here. These thoughts became a stronghold in her mind. She didn't feel valuable, or useful, she didn't see where she had any future. She felt defective and flawed. "I'll never do anything great anymore" she verbalized. She allowed these negative thoughts to sink into her head, heart and soul stifling her potential.

Overall, she was angry at God, her husband and the staff. These thoughts that she was wearing is what she became. She had a battle going on in her mind that was holding her back from moving forward. She was not progressing in her physical therapy. The therapists said she showed no progress and is not motived to participate in the treatment. She was not making headway in her counseling sessions, she didn't want to go outside for rides in the wheelchair van, she didn't want to listen to music, she didn't want to see movies she just wanted to die. She became what the negative thoughts in her mind were an unpleasant person to be around and not advancing to fulfill her destiny. These negative seeds were taking root and it was heartbreaking for Jack to see.

At this point she hated being in a wheelchair, she hated being in the nursing home, she hated the food, she hated the staff, she hated having to be dependent on others for her care, she hated life in general and wanted to check out.

Without delay, Jack knew he had to do something to change her mindset. He was aware that self-image was one of the key factors in success and happiness of an individual. He knew if Ann saw herself as unattractive, insignificant, inadequate, useless, inferior, she would act in accordance with her thoughts. If her self-worth is low, she will imagine she is a loser, washed out, unworthy of being loved and accepted. She believed she would never be happy or see good things in store for her in the future. These thoughts continued to dominate the conversations she had with Jack.

Of course, Jack wanted her to see herself a priceless treasure. Each day he went in to visit her once in the morning and once in the evening, he told her how much he loved her, how beautiful she was, and how much her son loved her. He told her she was strong, talented, creative, and good things were coming and that God has a specific purpose for her life. He told her that in order to achieve it she cannot think of herself as weak, sick lonely and defeated. He told her no matter how many setbacks she's had, she cannot accept that this is the way your life must be, as simply a survivor.

With this in mind, he flooded her with positive thoughts. He wanted to cast out the negative thoughts so she could begin to see herself as an overcomer, a winner, and to see herself as well able to see brighter days ahead.

Over and over he told her she was beautiful; she was valuable to him and her son. He told her what a great wife and mother she is, he told her God loved her and that good things were coming to them in time. He tried to enhance her self-esteem and confidence and to help her wipe out all the negative defeated thoughts she played over and over in her mind like a broken record.

Often, she engaged in negative political conversations. He was able to stop that negativity by refusing to talk politics. Her jealous obsession with Jack's past girlfriends dominated many of their conversations and he became firm with her and told her he was not going to engage in negative talk.

Specifically, he shifted the conversation to telling her how much he appreciated all she did for him when he was working and what a wonderful job, she did in raising their son, and how proud he is to be her husband. Overtime the belittling him about his past girlfriends and politics dissipated from their conversations.

However, the broken record of negative talk about the bum deal she received, and why God did this to her, and it's not fair that I had this stroke continued to be a focus in their daily conversations. She took two steps forward and regressed one step backwards.

Indeed, the negative talk was a huge challenge to turn around. It was exhausting and daunting for Jack as he made efforts to help her change her mind set. She has lived in a defeated mentality for over seven years, so Jack knew he had his work cut out for him. But he never lost focus, commitment, interest, or passion in trying to help Ann. This strategy of helping Ann clear her mind of negatives thoughts took place over a ten-month period.

With diligence and hard work on Jack's part the daily infusion of positive comments by Jack, he started to cast down the negative thoughts that Ann was engaged in. He tried to restore her faith in God by telling her that God had a specific purpose for her life and that he did not intend for her to go through life miserable, depressed, sick, and defeated.

Explicitly, he said to Ann "you may have been beaten down by the struggles of the stroke, but you do not have to be accustomed to being discouraged. You do not need to accept life far less than God's best". "God has better things in store for you Ann" he said, and "you do not need to drift through life haphazardly accepting whatever comes along, spinning your wheels till you die. You just have to have faith". He told her if she thinks little, believes little and expects little she will receive little. If you always think about defeat, failure, how weak you are and about how impossible your circumstances are you will never fulfill your destiny.

Truly, he worked hard to restore her faith in God. Overtime she started talking about God. She told Jack that her parents and his parents were all in heaven incredibly happy. She said his father was happy that he no longer had to pay bills. One day she told Jack that she saw Jesus with his arms wide open and He said to her, Ann you cannot come to heaven yet, you have to fulfill your destiny before you come.

Just when he thought he was making progress she reverted to the defeated mentality. He strived so hard to bring her to God and to lift her spirits. It was an up and down battle he fought every single day.

Jack developed a spiritual support plan for Ann. The plan had five components to it:

- Jack asked Ann's two best friends Audrey and Barbara if they could visit Ann more often since she enjoyed her two friends' visit so much. They visited each year for her birthday and her anniversary and provided a gala celebration for each event. Jack thought more frequent visits would lift Ann's spirits immensely

- and would give her something to look forward to.
- Jack asked the new Parish Priest if he could visit Ann more often since she found his visits greatly beneficial. The Priest made routine rounds at the home, but since his rectory where he lived was so close to the home Jack wondered if more frequent visits would be possible. He knew the visits would be helpful in keeping Ann's spirits and faith strong.
- He asked his son to call more often to lift her spirits.
- Jack explored with a local university that had a special education department if they could facilitate bussing in children with Downs syndrome to the home to visit with Ann and other residents. Ann had a special unique ability to bond and connect with children with downs syndrome during her prestigious career. Jack thought reinitiating that bond would lift her spirits dramatically. He also explored schools in the local area that taught downs syndrome children to ask them if they could initiate a program linking the special education children with the elderly in the nursing home. He plans to explore with Ann if she'd like to go to a local school in her wheelchair to work with special needs children. That would get her out of the home and interact with other people.
- Lastly, Jack requested to have Toby a service dog who bonded with Ann spend more time with Ann when the service dogs came to the home. She absolutely loved this one service dog Toby the best and received such joy on the days he visited.
- He requested mental health services from the psychologist assigned to the home.

## Implementing the Spiritual Support Plan

We all have an X factor or God's favor factor that gives us the energy, passion, and incentive to overcome obstacles so we can fulfill our destiny. In Ann's case her X factor is her passion to work with children with special needs. She has a God given talent to communicate, bond and empathize with special needs children.

To be sure, Jack wanted Ann to tap into her X factor to give her a sense of purpose, a sense of feeling valuable, a sense of passion to allow her to shake off the defeated mentality and fulfill her destiny. Working with special education children would give Ann a vision and a see a future for herself. It would wipe out her defeated mentality, uselessness, poor self-image, feeling unworthiness and lack of self-confidence. She could move forward from simply surviving to thriving. This connection with the children would move her toward feeling self-confident, useful, worthy, valuable, and passionate again.

For this reason, Jack had to figure out a way to accomplish this connection. He wasn't sure if taking her in a wheelchair to the school as a volunteer or having the children come to the home to do creative arts would be better. He planned to sit down with Ann and explore with her what her thoughts were.

With further thought, the option of having Ann go to the special education school was not feasible. Ann fatigued too easily and was not able to make the trips to the school. In addition, the home was not willing to drive her in a handicap van without charging an exorbitant fee. Jack could not afford the fee they charged to get her to the Board of Cooperative Educational Services, BOCES.

Consequently, Jack went to the Director of BOCES and asked if they could bus over some of the special education students to interact with the elderly residents. They came up with all kinds of excuses why that could not be accomplished. It's a liability issue what happens if the child gets injured sprains their ankle or contracts a disease such as the flu. What happens if the bus has an accident transporting the students? Who's going to pay for the transportation? The home refused to pay and so did BOCES. Jack asked why it couldn't be considered a field trip.

In particular, he outlined the benefits it would have for the students and the residents to the Director of BOCES. He presented it as a win/ win situation. The students would feel valued when the residents took an interest in them. The students would gain an appreciation of the elderly and the handicaps they are struggling with. They would feel a sense of accomplishment. The residents could help the students improve their social and academic skills.

For the residents it would enhance their feeling of self-worth they would feel valuable and useful again. The children's visits would lift their spirits and give them something to look forward to. But all this conversation fell on deaf ears. BOCES was out as an option.

With this in mind, he then went to a local university that had a special education department and asked if they could facilitate getting the special education children to visit in the nursing home. They said their purpose was to place their undergraduate and graduate students in a facility or school that had special education students. They set up practicums for the students to complete to become certified special education teachers, and that they did not place special education students in nursing homes. Their lack luster response was disappointing to Jack.

Not to be deterred Jack came up with the idea of contacting the director of special education at a local school about seven miles away. He met with the special education director and explained what his vision was and outlined his expected outcomes in term of residents and students. He explained he wanted to set up a best practice program entitled "Linking Special Education Students with Disabled Elderly."

Specifically, the students will bond with the residents they work with and a camaraderie and bonding will take place between the two. The students will come to recognize what an impact just their presence makes on the lives of others. The students will learn to appreciate others who are disabled and become more comfortable with residents with speech impediments, other disabilities, and foreign equipment such as oxygen tanks, drainage bags, braces, and other equipment.

Likewise, the residents working on creative arts, social skills, or reading skills with the students will feel valued, useful again, feel good about making a significant difference in the lives of others. The feeling of accomplishment will give the residents a sense of purpose to life and lift their spirits. The residents will rise above their pain and fatigue to be able to work with the special education students. It would be a Win / Win for both students and residents.

Surprisingly, the idea was well received, and a mutual agreement between the school and the nursing home was drafted up to bring the special education students to the home. The school agreed to transport the students into the home and back to the school. The students came to the home three times a week for two hours.

Jack was finally successful in getting Ann to connect with Downs Syndrome children in the nursing home. Ann bringing joy to the children improved her outlook. She was instrumental in improving the children's personal and social skills and this accomplishment built herself self-confidence.

On the positive side, the love and gratitude she received from the children had a positive influence on Ann and transformed her outlook on life. She was thinking in terms of others now and she felt useful and valuable once again. She made a difference in the lives of others which provided a sense of purpose and brought fulfillment to her life. This improved her happiness, built self-image which increased her psychological wellbeing.

Additionally, she was mentally stimulated and was thinking often of new strategies to help the children. She had a new vision, that expanded her horizons beyond the nursing home. Being physically and socially active and making significant contributions to the children, made her feel positive about herself and now viewed a life with a future and goals to meet.

Moreover, she made new friends with the students that gave her a new sense of energy. On bad days she rose above her pain and fatigue to work with the children knowing how much they looked forward to working with her. Working with the Downs Syndrome children turned her life around. She was no longer dwelling on her situation that was once filled with anger, resentment, bitterness, and hostility.

Significantly, the program linking Special Education students with elderly disabled residents in a nursing home setting was a huge success. They wrote the program up outlining the goals of the program and the benefits for both the students and the elderly were described. This was published in their nursing home newsletter and eventually submitted to a special education and nursing home journal for potential publication. The nursing home received calls from other nursing home facilities asking how they set the program up. Soon several nursing homes were replicating the program and obtaining similar outcomes.

The other parts of Jack's spiritual support plan were implemented also. Her friends Audrey and Barbara made more visits to Ann. Although it was difficult because they were getting up in age now, but they made special efforts to visit as often as possible.

Ann's calls came drifting in that she looked forward to and it made a huge difference in her mood. Her son was the apple of her eye and any contact with him made her feel exuberant. She was so ecstatic when a call was received.

Additionally, he had the psychologist talk with Ann on a set schedule. This part of the plan seemed to go well.

Markedly, Jack's efforts and love for Ann paid off. She was a completely new person. The resentment seething below the surface of every conversation she had with Jack was a thing of the past. Her defeated attitude and mentality that took a stronghold on her was released. She got rid of her former thoughts of defeat and failure. She enlarged her vision to see her doing something meaningful and achieving significance once again.

Notably, Ann was no longer locked in self-pity. She did not let her disability defeat her. She took the strength that God armed her with and trained her mind to see the good and to be grateful for what she had. She learned to be content in her situation. She began to see herself as beautiful, strong, talented, and valuable.

Moreover, she recognized that God was at work in her life. She developed an attitude of faith and now expects events to change positively. She lived with expectancy, had bigger dreams, prayed big and made room in her thinking for the things God wants her to do. It was nothing less than an extraordinary miracle! Jack the mighty hero never gave up on his wife and his motto is Never Give Up!

# *10*

# THE CORONAVIRUS HITS THE WORLD...

**INTRODUCTION TO CORONA PANDEMIC**

JUST WHEN THINGS were going well with Jack and Ann the corona epidemic hits the U.S. An invisible enemy has hit our nation and the world. This is a challenging time for our nation, taken down by an invisible enemy that is threatening our harm, safety, economy, and community. Our tools for combatting this as a nation are courage, compassion, and kindness, as we help each other through this crisis. We are using technology to connect with one another as we are being tested. Our resolve, compassion, sacrifice, empathy and simple kindness is critical for national recovery.

Markedly, the disease is taking out our citizens breath and life at record high numbers. Our heart goes out to the health care workers risking their own lives putting themselves in harm's way to care for the ill. We are incredibly grateful to them. The suffering we are witnessing and experiencing for the for ill, unemployed, frontline workers, and elderly is heartbreaking.

Sadly, the hugs and kisses we once embraced are now seen as harmful and frightening. Seeing grandma and grandpa is no longer possible for fear of bringing the virus to them. Visiting loved ones in nursing homes and hospitals is restricted. We must stay six feet away from each other called social distancing with no social embraces other than a smile. Our whole world is turned upside down. We must not let the physical distance create and emotional distance.

Officials at all levels are putting forth guidelines for us to follow to keep us safe. As these guidelines are developed, we find the nation turned upside down. Specifically, health care workers were running extremely low on personal protective equipment and were using garbage bags as gowns and handmade masks. In fact, elective surgery was prohibited since all resource's gowns, masks and personnel were being directed to caring for patients suffering with corona. People in severe pain unable to walk had to postpone their knee replacement surgery. Cancer patients' treatments were put on hold. Truckers delivering vital supplies to grocery stores and healthcare facilities could not park their trucks and secure food at truck stops. Likewise, all businesses were shut down the unemployment rate was rising. The economy was tanking to an all-time low.

Notably, the nation was in shock, but the citizens thought we have faced tough times as a nation before and have risen above the storm to become victorious. We must not let fear and loneliness take over our spirit. We learned from the past that our sacrifice and spirit to serve brought us together as a nation. We learned that empathy and kindness and care for others was what allowed us to get through the crisis. We are all vulnerable and wonderful and will get through this together. We must put our political differences aside and face this together.

However, little did the citizens know that as the pandemic progressed that it would turn into a political firestorm with people unable to put their political differences aside.

## Corona Pandemic Hits Jack Directly

This crisis hit Jack personally. He received a call from the nursing home informing him that the corona epidemic hit the state of New York badly, and to prevent Corona from spreading throughout the nursing home a no visitor plan was put in place. Thus the student program Jack initiated was terminated.

Thus, nursing home volunteers, special needs students, family members, entertainment people, hairdressers were all barred from visiting. He could call Ann on an appointment basis and speak to her. When he called, he reassured her he was doing fine and told her he loved her and missed her.

Slowly, without the volunteers, her service dog visits and Jack not visiting Ann's spirits began to decline again. She was talking once again about wanting to die, how she hated the nursing home, how she hated the food, she hated the wheelchair, she hated the staff and hated life in general. A major setback in Ann's spirits.

Of course, Ann's attitude and the coronavirus were unsettling for Jack. He was worried about delivery people and staff bringing the corona into the home. He knew that once it got into the nursing home it would spread like wildfire.

At this time, he expressed his concerns to the nursing home administrator. They reassured him they were following all the CDC guidelines and all staff and delivery people had their temperatures taken before entering the home.

Undoubtedly, not convinced this was enough Jack was very worried. Soon he received a letter stating four residents came down with the corona virus but were on the other side of the home from where Ann was located. Once again, they tried to reassure him that they were following all the recommendations and guidelines from CDC.

Subsequently, four weeks passed with no visits. Only phone calls by appointment. This was his only contact Jack had with Ann. He spoke with her one morning and she said she felt fine and was doing OK. He was delighted with that phone call that seemed upbeat on Ann's part.

However, that afternoon he received a phone call that Ann ran a fever and tested positive for the corona virus. He was informed four more patients had the virus and they were all placed in isolation, including Ann.

Indeed, he is devastated and genuinely concerned knowing with her age and underlying atrial fibrillation condition that statistics suggest that she was extremely high risk for a disastrous outcome. He knew her atrial fibrillation condition, controlled with medication, may make her ineligible to be considered for the experimental Hydroxychloroquine with Zithromax.

First and foremost, Jack had his son call to ask the nursing home to put her on the experimental drug. His son had more mental speed and could talk and think faster on his feet than Jack and was able to ask return questions and counter what they were saying with a clear mind.

Despite their request, the home said at this point she's not exhibiting any other symptoms and she is not going to be placed on any medication.

Meanwhile, Jack waits and prays his heart out that she will pull through. He was concerned that with her lack of will to live she may just give up and die. Each day that went by he waited for the dreadful call that she was starting to exhibit symptoms of cough and shortness of breath. Each time his phone rang he'd have an adrenaline flush just knowing it was the nursing home calling with bad news. He couldn't sleep and now he was experiencing severe anxiety and pain. He was in a state of anticipatory grief.

Meanwhile, he contacted his friend Mary to tell her the news about Ann. Mary tried to give him some words of comfort. She told him that he had to turn these unfair things over to God. "God will fight your battle" she said. "God knows what you and Ann need. Leave the door wide open to for God to do the right thing". Mary said she felt confident that God had a plan for both and Jack should put all the issues in God's hands.

To clarify, she went on to say, "You've done all you know how to do Jack, she said, and He will take your horrendous battlefield and turn it into a blessing field. Have faith Mary said. You are being hit by a horrific storm that you will be able to withstand it".

Then, she reminded him of the palm tree story that Joel Osteen talked about. She said, "Just like the palm tree bent way over flattened to the ground, looking as if life is gone forever during a strong storm, it was in fact only in temporary defeat and after the storm it rose in victory."

In order to encourage him, Mary told Jack he had the ability to weather the storm and that he will spring back like the palm tree. God made you to withstand the storm even the most difficult of storms. You are a fighter and will survive. Mary reminded Jack of Psalm 46 God is present to help in times of need.

As she spoke, he listened, but made no comment. In a state of shock, she was not sure he processed what she said and did not know if her words were comforting or annoying.

At the end of their conversation he did ask her if he could talk with her periodically to relieve his stress. She said she would be happy to be there for him whenever he needed to talk.

In due time, Mary and Jacks next conversation surrounded talking about the various medications being used in China, South Korea, and the ones that clinical trials were testing. They talked about other treatment modalities being used. He praised Trump for all the work he was doing in fast tracking the clinical trials and getting the FDA to approve emergency use of Hydroxychloroquine for patients with corona right now.

Specifically, he wanted to know about what drugs looked promising. Mary explained that the two most promising drugs at this time that are being used under compassionate use was Hydroxychloroquine with Zithromax and Remdesivir.

In detail, she explained that many antiviral drugs were being tested such as HIV drugs Kaletra, Lopimune, Lopinavir, and Ritahavir. Also, human plasma derived products were being tested. Synair an inhaled drug was being looked at. Other anti virals being investigated were Favilavir, Infenprodil, Regeneron plus Kevzara, Brilacidin, and Galidesivir.

Additionally, Mary mentioned they had many lab and universities trying to develop a vaccine, but it would take up to a year before that was completed and tested for safety. He was disappointed that so many were in trial taking months to finish and he wanted something for Ann, now.

Following that conversation news was coming out how they were pilot testing antibody infusions to patients with corona from patients who recovered from corona. The drug Remdesivir a medication used for Ebola patients was now showing some promise for patients on ventilators. It was administered Intravenously. Other institutions were testing an inhalation modality of llama antibodies thought to help disarm the corona. Johnson and Johnson and a study in Oxford England were both on the forefront of developing a vaccine by 2021.

Specifically, he wanted to know when Ann may start to show symptoms after the fever she exhibited. Mary told Jack the most common symptoms were cough, sore throat, fatigue, headache, and shortness of breath progressing to extreme difficulty in breathing. Some were coming down with conjunctivitis. This virus was a true lung eater.

In this case, Mary's best prediction was five days after the fever some of the symptoms may appear. She had the fever on Saturday, so Thursday was when they expected the symptoms to appear.

Indeed, waiting for Thursday to come he found himself totally exhausted talking to all of Ann's friends on the phone who were requesting updates on Ann. He was on the phone with family and friends all day. He was bone weary.

It must be remembered that now because she is on isolation, he can't even talk with her on the phone. He was wondering if he was ever going to be able to see her again since he was not able to visit her. He hasn't seen her now in over a month since the home restricted all visitors. He thought over in his mind the last visit and conversation he had with her. It played in his mind over and over.

During this time, the dreadful memories of when she was hospitalized with encephalitis leading to the stroke eight years ago started tormenting him. He was in an unbelievably bad place, so sad and lonely and worried. It was awful. His son was in California and only spoke with him on the phone. Jack felt so all alone.

Hence, Thursday finally came, and sure enough Ann had a cough and was not eating. Jack and Jack, Jr, his son from California both called and insisted she be on the Hydroxychloroquine, Zithromax, and Zinc cocktail. They were extremely persistent because Jack knew once the congestion and the cytokine inflammatory storm set in Ann would go down the tubes for sure.

Finally, the home said they would have the physician examine her health records for placement on the hydroxy cocktail. The physician ordered it and she was started on it right away. They were so relieved she was approved for the medication.

As a result, in two days, her cough stopped, and she was eating again. It was like a miracle. She of course remained in isolation.

Henceforth, he called daily and they said she was doing well. This was good news for Jack. After two weeks of getting good reports Jack and his son wanted to hear from Ann how she was doing. Jack's son insisted on talking with her and the home set up a conference call for Jack and his son to talk with her.

While on the conference call they were able to tell her they loved her, were thinking about her, and wanted her to get well. They reassured her that they were safe and well. She was quiet during the conference call, but said she was feeling ok. Both Jack and his son were happy for the call and felt relieved that she was doing well.

To clarify, several days later Jack called to make sure they were getting Ann up and out of bed for fear that pneumonia would set in if left lying in bed all day.

Because of his concern, they put him through to Ann's nurse who was a new nurse caring for Ann. The nurse was the kindest person Jack ever encountered. She took a picture of Ann, with Ann's permission to send to Jack and put Ann on the phone to speak with him. Ann was upbeat and positive saying she is receiving physical therapy. She was optimistic in saying she is going to walk again. Of course, Jack knew that was not going to happen, but was delighted with her optimism and good mood.

Of course, Jack knew that being in denial is sometimes a good thing because it makes one work harder during the physical therapy sessions and gives one hope to keep moving forward.

As a matter of fact, Ann loved the new nurse. Jack thanked the nurse profusely for her kindness and for going the extra mile in sending him a picture of Ann and for letting him talk with her.

After the visit, when he got home, he called his son immediately to give him the good news about Ann's mood and shared the picture with him. Jack Jr. was so happy to hear the good news.

While Jack is at home, he is very lonely. With the stay at home order and not being able to visit Ann, he began to wonder when he will ever see Ann again.

At this time, two months have gone by and he has not visited her. Now the lock down was ordered for the state of New York. He has not seen anybody due to the lock down. All restaurants were now closed. He goes out to get takeout for his meals and that's the only time he sees any civilization.

However, one day on his way to get takeout food he saw his neighbor and waved. He stopped to ask her how she was doing, and she broke down in tears. She said her brother was in the ICU on a ventilator with corona and was not doing well. She was living with her 92-year-old dad who was distraught over his son being so sick. Jack wanted to get out to give her a hug to comfort her, but could not do it because of social distancing. He told her he was so sorry and to keep him posted.

As each day passed Jack was getting down in his spirits, so lonely with no one to talk with and worried sick about Ann. He missed his son who lived in California and was worried about him staying safe and healthy. Life for Jack was very dispiriting at this point.

Moreover, he received daily calls from his sister Audrey that were so depressing for Jack. His sister has diabetes that is not controlled. She had bad cataracts and cannot see. She is financially strapped and has a husband that is verbally abusing her. Their home is now in foreclosure because she can't pay the mortgage. Jack feels helpless and can only help by listening and giving her advice. His sister's situation and the concern of Ann has Jack pretty stressed out.

To offset this negativity, he kept in touch with Mary, Coach Rocco, his sister Ellen, and friend Justin to see how they were doing. This at least gave him an opportunity to talk with someone more positive.

As a result, he learned from Justin that a co-worker at the bag shop where Justin worked died of corona. He also learned that one of Jack's friends and his wife both had corona. This couple has a disabled child and Jack was worried about the child. Justin did not know who was taking care of the child with both parents struggling with corona. He told Justin he was worried about him and told him to stay safe. The bag shop was considered essential, so Justin went into work every day.

Next, he called his former Coach now 93 who lived with his daughter. Jack learned that he got out in his yard every day for about an hour and spent his time reading a book about Yogi Berra. Coach Rocco missed seeing the Yankees play baseball and looked forward to when the games would resume. He reassured Jack he was doing well.

Although the calls were not long in duration, he did feel better after talking with them. The one bright light in his life was his sister Ellen who is always upbeat and positive. She always had interesting stories and news to share with Jack that uplifted his spirits. She keeps busy by renovating portions of her home. The latest was the dining room that turned out to be beautiful. Ellen is always a breath of fresh air to talk with.

At this point, Mary was doing fine with the lockdown. In fact, initially it was refreshing not having to be anywhere at any given time. She slept in and was enjoying spending more time with her husband and dog. Jack enjoyed Mary's calls too.

Surprisingly, the next day, Jack got the bad news that his neighbor's brother died in the hospital. After being on the ventilator for five days fighting for his life with corona, he died.

Straightaway, Jack got so choked up seeing the grief in her eyes all he could get out was "I'm so sorry". Jack was so distraught and wanted to give her a hug but restrained himself. His neighbor now had to not only deal with the loss of her brother, but had to deal with her dad's grief as well.

At this time, Jack now has two friends that died of corona, two who are struggling to stay alive with the corona and his wife in the nursing home who thank God is recovering well from corona.

In the meantime, his son was trying not only to cheer his mom up, but his dad too. The burden on Jack, Jr. was horrendous. Living in California and his parents in New York was particularly difficult for him.

In due time Jack called his friend Mary and his sister Ellen again to keep his sanity. Both were encouraging and he felt support from both.

But, two days later he received a call from his friend Justin that so many of Jack's former coworkers came down with corona at the bag shop. Justin is exhausted picking up their workload. They are running short staffed and Justin wonders how long it will be before the bag shop has to shut down. The work they do is very specialized and requires extensive training to perform the machinery.

Despite all the misery surrounding Jack, he refuses to retreat into his cave again. Missing the visits with his wife, getting news that all around him neighbors, former work colleagues and friends are coming down with the corona virus was discouraging to say the least, but he stayed strong.

After all, he was a veteran cave dweller for seven years and living in isolation was now not difficult for him like others. He was determined not to let this setback get him down. In fact, he sang his song *"No More Cave for Me"* that helped keep his spirits up.

At the present time, he gets his food through drive through establishments, washes his clothes by hand since his washing machine is broken and the laundromats are closed. He writes poems, songs, listens to music and the news to keep informed and reads great books. Jack was handling the lock down very well.

### The Nation Retreats into the Cave

The whole country is now retreating into the cave. The media was less than optimistic. They bombarded everyone with the bad news of corona. They give the doom and gloom news 24/7 that we are all going to die if we don't stay in the cave chained to the wall lying in a fetal position till there's a vaccine developed, projected to be accomplished in a year.

In view of the situation, people were terrified and worried about having cardiac episode not wanting to go to the hospital for fear of contacting the corona virus. They prayed that they would not have any dental emergency for fear if they had it taken care of, they would come down with the corona virus.

As a matter of fact, people in New York where Jack lived were told they cannot go outside to feel the sun beaming down on their backs, to hear the birds sing, to feel the wind blow against their face, to smell the flowers. They could not go outside to see the squirrels frolicking around the trees chasing each other across the lawns. All the things we took for granted suddenly came to a screeching halt.

Consequently, people in other states during the lock down were arrested for being in the wide-open lake on their motor boats, fathers were being arrested playing catch with their sons in an open vacant baseball field, people were being fined $1,000.00 dollars, for not wearing masks that no one can secure.

Moreover, people wanting to paint the inside of their house during lockdown could not buy paint in a store that was opened such as Walmart, Sam's Club and BJ's. They could only buy the food in that store, not paint. Paint was considered a non-essential item.

Further, one woman with a child was aggressively approached about her not wearing her mask properly. It didn't cover her entire nose. When she tried to pull the police officer's hands off her arm she was thrown to the ground in front of her child and arrested.

In fact, in New York City the Mayor gave out a phone number for citizens to snitch on their neighbors if they found they were outside or not wearing a mask or were not practicing the social distancing.

Surprisingly, a friend of Mary's who lived in New York had a porch that was falling apart. Two men came to help her restore the porch. They were approached by the police because a neighbor called that number and reported that the two men were not practicing social distancing. They were too close to each other as the hammered the wood. They were told by the police that only one man could work on the porch. To finish the porch, it required two men. Thus, the porch was left unfinished and was a safety hazard for Mary's elderly friend.

Also, people were arrested for travelling by car to visit family members who were bringing food to their elderly parents. In like fashion people were arrested for attending a church service in an open lot in their cars while watching the preacher on a televised large screen

In addition, one woman was threatened by the police because she let her child out on the front lawn to play with her supervision. The police said she and the child must stay within the confines of her home, not outside. Another person was planting vegetables in their garden and was told they could not do that. A neighbor's teenage child was cutting their lawn and the teenager was told to stay in the home and was emphatic that he had to stay inside.

Moreover, a single mom worried about feeding her children opened her hair salon following the social distance guidelines and requiring masks was arrested and forced to apologize to the judge for being selfish in not following the stay at home order. She refused to apologize and was sentenced to stay in jail for one week where they had inmates with corona virus. Meanwhile, her children had no mom for a week.

Markedly, many citizens believed the draconian restrictions placed on citizens by government officials and were violating individuals' constitutional rights in every way imaginable. Restrictions were based on reasons that were not supported by scientific data. Citizens are trapped in the cave with no sense of realty. Their only perspective on realty is the walls in their home. Just like Plato's Cave.

At this time, the unemployment rate was unbelievably high. People were not being able to work to put food on the table for their family. Their bills were piling up with no income. Unemployment rates were over three million. People were contemplating suicide, drinking themselves to death. The isolation was intolerable for most and depression was setting in on the vulnerable. Children were bouncing off the walls since schools and day care centers were closed.

For the most part, moms who did work had childcare issues and moms that were at home were responsible for home schooling their children. Having children at three and four different grade levels made this challenging. The parents were stressed to the maximum. The stress placed on these parents was unbelievable. Jack couldn't imagine how parents trying to work, home school their multi- grade level children and worried about how their elderly parents were surviving.

Sadly, health care workers were suffering from post-traumatic syndrome filled with anxiety, anger, and a feeling of helplessness. They were not only seeing their patients dying on ventilators, but were worried about their family contacting the corona from them. They slept in cars so they would not expose their family to the corona they may be carrying on their clothes.

Overall, all cleaning supplies Lysol, Clorox, hand sanitizer, and isopropyl alcohol were impossible to obtain. Nobody could figure out why toilet paper was scarce. People were fighting in the aisles of grocery stores for toilet paper. After the toilet paper fights in the grocery stores and obtaining takeout food it was back to the cave for many.

So, the only outside contact people had was via phone or computerized visual conference calls such as zoom, or skype where people could connect with family and friends and see each other. Younger adults were using House Party an online application on Friday nights to connect with five or six couples to play games online and allowed them to see each other while playing the games. This provided them with at least some social interaction.

But many did not have the technology to set up the computerized visualized conference calls, zoom or House Party. These individuals were totally isolated. Depression and loneliness were setting in the people with no technology capability. Many of these people had signs in their windows: Need More Wine! They hoped some kind soul would go out and get them a bottle of wine to numb their loneliness.

In the meantime, no one could have weddings, funerals, sporting events, concerts, birthday, anniversary celebrations or any momentous celebrations unless in was in the confines of the cave.

During this time, the nursing home residents and assisted care elderly residents were suffering from extreme isolation and loneliness. It was unbearable for them to be locked up in the cave with no visitors, volunteers, or therapy dogs or mail for three months. Many nursing home residents started to show signs of failing to thrive from lack of social interaction.

While confined to the cave the uncertainty and stress was relentless and painful. The mental strain was horrendous. All one could see on Facebook, TV or listen to on the radio were commentators talking about issues such as: Do you take your shoes off when you come back from grocery store? Do you take your clothes off immediately and change into other clothes? Do you wash your grocery milk cartons, egg boxes and salad bags of with disinfectant wipes? Can you eat out of takeout order containers or do they have to be put immediately on your plates and containers discarded. Do you wipe down your mail?

At the same time, teaching demonstrations on how to make masks out of bras, scarfs, tee shirts, and jock straps were shown on Facebook, since masks were unavailable to obtain.

Maddening was the fact that information on how long the virus lasts on paper, plastic, wood, counter tops, and cardboard was discussed incessantly. Each time it was presented it conflicted with the day before report.

All this information on mask making, handling one's mail and groceries and how long the virus lasts on surfaces was overwhelming, mind boggling and exasperating.

Subsequently, the rest of the nation was in the cave suffering from stress of the unknown, from the severe isolation, and fear of contacting the virus. They were angry at China for their deception, angry that we were so dependent on them for our medical supplies and medication. This anger coupled with fear was paralyzing citizens physically and mentally.

As time passed by the citizens were overwhelmed with the news that kept changing. The data of how many were ill, how many died, the guidelines of wearing masks how long the virus stayed on various surfaces changed every five minutes. When the vaccine would be ready was not clear and recommendations of what is the preferred treatment was very conflicting and changing every day. Answers to questions about whether it is air borne or not depended on who the last health expert was now pontificating on the subject. The entire nation was in lock down suffering in their cave.

## Corona Cave

*(Poem written describing how Jack felt at the time)*

*There is a cave down lonely street I have been there once before*
*Now I am back there once again corona at the door*
*But I was saved one other time an angel friend to me*
*She helped me get out of here to smile again and be free*
*We all got cooped up the virus yes indeed*
*And now we need to live again get the country up to speed*
*So, we all will emerge the caves no place to be*
*And people can get back to work the place they ought to be*
*So next time we will be ready and plan you see*
*And put our trust in ourselves do not depend on overseas*
*We see what they can do to us full of their disease*
*So, let's hope our politicians can see between the trees*
*And change the way we do business bring them to their knees*

*Author:* Pete Delmonico

### Jack's Friend Mary Retreats to the Cave

Jack's friend Mary, is now, to his surprise finding her change in lifestyle, and the dreadful news about the virus difficult. She is a very social person used to going to the orchestra, meeting friends for lunch, attending conferences, and attending reunions. She is missing her massages, haircuts, pedicures, and shopping sprees. Most of all she misses seeing her son and all her hugs from him and friends.

Surprisingly, she retreated into the cave now along with everyone in the country. Jack is concerned. The roles have now reversed. Jack comes to Mary's aid to help her come out of the cave living in misery. He sends her sweet encouraging poems and reminds Mary of her strong faith and her never give up attitude. He is now trying hard to rescue Mary from the cave.

Under the circumstances she felt guilty complaining to Jack when she thought of all the families who lost their jobs and were not able to put food on the table for their family. She thought of all the health care workers putting themselves in harm's way and all the patients fighting for their lives from the aggressive corona virus. Her guilt was relentless. Her anxiety was overwhelming. She worried about the uncertainty of everything and all the conflicting information received on the news.

More importantly, she worried that if she or her family got the corona, she now would not be able to get the hydroxychloroquine cocktail that Jacks wife got, because they were not allowing physicians to order it now. One had to be in the hospital to receive it and many patients were getting it too late for it to work. Hydroxychloroquine must be given before the congestion and inflammation cytokine storm occurred for it to be effective. They were giving it to patients once they were on ventilators and of course by then it was too late. So many concluded the medication did not work.

Explicitly, the FDA now recommended it had to be given under the supervision of a physician in a hospital setting and this concerned Mary. The FDA said the drug could possibly have some cardiac effects.

This rendered family physicians impotent to order hydroxychloroquine for their patients right away that would keep them out of the hospital.

It's well known that Tylenol can cause severe liver disease, but that is Ok to take. Aspirin, Aleve, and Advil can cause severe gastrointestinal bleeding, but that's Ok to take. Statin drugs have critical life-threatening muscular side effects, but that's Ok to take. Metformin had drastic kidney side effects, but that was Ok to take. Every single medication has potential side effects.

In fact, hydroxychloroquine had been given for years to patients with lupus and rheumatoid arthritis for over fifty years with very little side effects and no reports of patients dying

Sadly, the hydroxychloroquine became a political issue thus the FDA recommended that patients receive the medication only in the hospital under medical supervision. Although it was just a recommendation the governors were denying primary care physicians from ordering the medication for their patients forcing the patients to be admitted to the hospital to receive it.

This order from Governors enraged Mary and created a tremendous source of anxiety for her. She feared her family would receive it too late and being forced to go to the hospital would unnecessarily expose them to not only corona, but other hospital acquired infections such as staph infections, TB and other infections putting them at perilous risk.

It appeared that the use of this age-old drug used for years with very few incidences of adverse reactions was being politized for some reason. This drove Mary crazy. This was a horrendous situation and concern that Mary was struggling with.

Expressly, Jack told Mary he was concerned about her and that she needed to use her talents and help the nurses putting themselves in harm's way. He hoped this would take her mind off the worries she had and perhaps she could come out of the cave and stop living in misery. He was confident with her skills she would make a significant contribution to helping those caring for the patients.

So, Mary thought about it and came up with an idea how to help the nurses. She called the nursing administration at the local hospital where she used to work and told the administrator she wants to help 20 nurses with food delivery, babysitting, laundry, and toys for children at home. The administrator who Mary knew gave her the names of 20 nurses with their permission.

Specifically, Mary contacted vendors to deliver groceries to their home every two weeks, had laundromat facilities agree to pick up their dirty laundry outside the home wash it and return it to the home. She had bakeries deliver cookies to the homes for the children and toys stores to donate toys for the children. Many these vendors were closed during the lockdown, but Mary got them to agree to deliver the items and services requested. She tried to get friends of hers that were solid citizens to babysit the children while Mom was at work. This was the most difficult part because people did not want to go in the homes afraid, they would get corona. So, the nurses had to rely on relatives or friends of theirs to watch the children.

Markedly, Mary spent hours online texting, emailing, and calling vendors requesting their services and donations. Finally, she took care of all 20 nurses. She needed a break now. So, Jack told her to recruit 10 nurses and train them on how to do what she did. He suggested to have each of them work with 20 nurses. That would be 200 nurses taken care of. And now Mary could serve as a consultant to the 10 nurses. That is exactly what she did. The project was extraordinarily successful.

As a result, the nurses, when they came home exhausted, now did not have to do grocery shopping or laundry. The children had fresh new toys to keep them occupied and cookies for a treat.

In any event, Jack had a very calming effect on Mary and finally with his delightful poems, encouraging words and keeping her busy with the nurses' project she came out of the cave. She stayed strong and continued to look for opportunities to help others. As she came out of the cave, she put her worries in the hand of God. She continued to look for opportunities to help others suffering in the cave as well as the nurses putting themselves in harm's way caring for those struggling with corona. Jack was very content, happy that he lured Mary out of the cave.

## Jack's Birthday Celebration

During the lock down Jack celebrated his 77th birthday in isolation by himself. He got a card from his son, Mary, and Ellen. He received several calls from friends wishing him a happy birthday. And he received a call from his wife's nurse knowing it was his birthday. She put his wife Ann on the phone so she could sing happy birthday to him. After she sung happy birthday to him, she told him she loved him and that she was doing fine. She wished him a happy birthday again, and they hung up the phone.

Indeed, this was the best birthday present he could have ever received. He was so happy and on cloud nine hearing from his wife. He remarked that it does not get any better than that. He was thrilled to hear from her, and his birthday was very joyful. A great day for him.

### Birthday Poem

*(Poem written about Jack's birthday)*

*I had a birthday as big a bash as could be*
*But no one showed up I was all alone*
*I was all alone just me*
*Not anyone could come near me*
*Corona was the Chinese present thank God it did not reach me*
*So thankful for the shutdown the virus I don't need*
*So, they can take the their present and stick it up their sleeve*
*They have played us for suckers*
*And yes, it is world war three*
*I hope that we get even with trade, not going to be*

*And let them sell deceitful stuff to someone else not me*
*As we get back to normal whenever that may be*
*We must be much wiser with Trump I do agree*
*The politicians in this country are not smart enough to see*
*That China is our enemy*
*No friend does that you see*
*So, when we open again the country will unfreeze*
*And release the greatest economy the world will ever see*

*Author: Pete Delmonico*

Without a doubt, Jack had a good birthday and was handling the pandemic restrictions and isolation simply fine. His wife completely recovered from Corona and he was not feeling the stress of isolation and lock down as others were experiencing. He looked at the lock down as an opportunity to get some extra prayer time in, to write poems and songs, listen to music, connect with friends by phone and text. He got some extra needed sleep in feeling more refreshed and was incredibly positive in his outlook.

### DRACONIAN RESTRICTIONS BEING CHALLENGED BY CITIZENS

Jack wondered at times what's scarier than the corona is the unprecedented over reach of local authorities in dominating every aspect of one's life from travel, to assembly, to earning a living, to hours one can stay outside, to what you are allowed to buy or worship. The erosion of these most basic rights was intolerable.

Finally, after 60 days of being on lock down some citizens started challenging the draconian restrictions and the science presented used as a basis for the lockdown. People felt their liberties were being violated and started protesting in several states. They wanted their business to open. Restaurant owners, beauty parlors and retail stores were opening and defying the restrictions. People were going to the closed parks, beaches and hiking trails defying the restrictions to stay home. They wore masks and followed the social distancing guidelines and continued to wash their hands but refused to be told by government officials that they had to stay home lying in fetal position till the vaccine was developed.

Over time, the federal lock down was now lifted, and the states were now in charge of making decisions as to when they would lift the restrictions. Each state was charged with developing an implementation plan for lifting restrictions on what could be opened.

As the curve flattened out ,the states who respected peoples choices, rights and desires to return to work ,opened restaurants, and retail stores, resumed elective surgery, lifted the restrictions in waves to allow people to return to some degree of normalcy. However, other states claimed they wanted to continue with restrictions for people's safety. And refused to lift the restrictions till there was a vaccine.

Consequently, this led to the protesting group believing they continued the restrictions to ensure the economy would tank before the upcoming election. In fact, some governors clung on to their draconian restrictions violating peoples' constitutional rights so bad that the Attorney General had to initiate investigations and start litigation processes.

In essence, it was believed by many that there was an election coming up and the media and left-wing proponents wanted the economy to be stagnant in hopes of ousting Trump. The media did ridicule anyone protesting for their rights to be reinstalled. They planted protesters with swath stickers and confederate flags in the protestors groups to make them look bad. The protestors were called Nazis and racist.

Overall, it was hard to believe in time of crisis that politicians would not put aside their political differences and do whatever was right for the nation. The pandemic has seemed to divide the nation even further apart than before the corona virus hit.

At this time, the protesters wanted to get back to work to provide for their family. Many wanted to get back to worshipping in their cars with the pastor on a stage to conduct the service. Staying in their cars honored the social distancing. Others wanted haircuts, pedicures, massages and wanted to go to the gym to workout.

Furthermore, many wanted their recreation activities to be restored so they could go to the beach, hiking, boating, and fishing. Some just wanted to have a meal in a restaurant that followed the social distance and CDC cleaning guidelines.

Clearly, these people were emphatic and were not going to let government influence that goal and take away their liberties protected by the constitution. All protestors followed and embraced the masks, social distancing guidelines and hand washing in a responsible fashion. But, they were not going to stay at home scared to death, living in fear, and lying in an embryonic state till there was a vaccine available.

## JACK USED HIS TIME WISELY DURING LOCK DOWN

While all this chaos was going on in the country Jack decided to spend some time trying to figure out how to get Ann reconnected to the special needs children to lift her spirits. The children were not permitted to go visit the patients in person, so Jack had to come up with a creative way to connect her to the children.

Specifically, he explored online virtual tutor where Ann may be able to talk to and read to the children online. He investigated Virtual Volunteering another online application to connect with the children. He researched Vello online reading program and skype, zoom and an application called House Party where one can connect with others and play games. He developed a plan to discuss with the activity director when she was allowed to return to the home. The plan included how to develop activities for the residents using technology.

## Jack Kept Up on New Treatments that Continued to Evolve:

Jack was delighted to hear the news now coming out on how they were pilot testing antibody infusions to patients with corona from patients who recovered from corona. The drug Remdesivir a medication used for Ebola patients was touted that it was now showing promise for patients. It was administered Intravenously. But in fact, overtime clinical trial showed it was not so helpful in treating patients with corona who were on ventilators. It seemed that Remdesivir worked better early in the onset of corona. A drug called Ivermectin used to treat parasites lick lice was showing some promise in treating the corona virus.

Jack kept up with the news related to the institutions that were testing an inhalation modality of llama antibodies thought to help disarm the corona. He listened daily for news on the progress of the Johnson and Johnson and a study and Oxford England who were both developing a vaccine. He learned that Israel was testing a drug that was having huge success in treating the cytokine inflammation storm for those patients who were extremely sick with the virus.

Each day new innovations were being reported. But none came close to working as well as hydroxychloroquine at the time. Yale University completed a clinical trial controlled and found that hydroxychloroquine with Tocilizumab was effective if given to patients as soon as symptoms appeared. It was recommended that every family practitioner should consider prescribing this combo to patients as soon as they tested positive for corona. But critics of that drug continued on the forefront trying to discredit the drug.

The medical profession was now in non-agreement about the use of hydroxychloroquine. Physicians who agreed it worked well did a y tube video that was barred from being seen. It was taken down arbitrarily with no explanation of why. And other physicians who were not proponents of hydroxychloroquine were on TV saying how it did not work. It was shocking how this one drug became so politized.

### Jack Felt Sad That the Nation was Divided into Two Groups

At this time, the country was now divided between two opposing groups. Namely, one group who retreated in their cave depressed, angry and bitter, and the other group that challenged the lockdown and the science behind the polices.

Specifically, the protestors who wanted to escape from the cave of lockdown stood strong with courage, conviction and made choices that they felt were in their family's best interest. They escaped the cave and were bringing joy back to their lives and working hard to become prosperous once again. People were going to the beaches, getting out on their boats, eating in restaurants, getting haircuts, shopping in retail stores, jogging on hiking trails and parks.

However, the cave dwellers remained chained in the cave feeling depressed, bitter, angry, and miserable. They had hair growing down to their shoulders, were drinking a lot and terrified to go outside to breathe some fresh air. They were overly reliant on the media and government official's information that some believed was propaganda and brainwashing. Viewing the news 24/7 resulted in lack of courage, strength, and confidence in their ability to escape the cave. They lived in constant fear and became totally helpless in rising above all the conflict and terror. They bought the idea that they had to stay home chained in the cave till a vaccine was developed.

Overall, the media was being accused of purposively instilling fear among citizens and using propaganda and lies to support their ideology. In fact, it was a common belief among the protestors that the left-wing media did everything they could to intimidate people, instill fear in them so they'd stay in the cave till after the election helping the economy to remain stagnant. It was believed by the protestors that this was their last-ditch effort to defeat Trump in November.

All in all, the group that stayed at home till there is a vaccine labeled the protesters racist, Nazi's. They accused the protesters of being irresponsible, selfish, and said all the people would die if they went outside.

Likewise, the protester groups called the stay at home group "Anti Trumpers". They accused the cave dwellers of purposely trying to tank the economy so Trump would lose the election. They labeled them of anti-American.

Ultimately, the cave dwellers maintained they were following the media and the government officials, because they wanted to stay safe and protect others from getting ill. But protestor group maintained it was a well-orchestrated strategy to take down Trump because many of the restrictions were not based on accurate scientific data. They pointed out how the data and scientific recommendations changed every other day. It's air borne one day, next day it's not, masks are critical one day, next day maybe not so critical, it's on all surfaces everything has to be washed off, next day no it doesn't stay on surfaces as long as we thought, and one doesn't have to wash down mail and groceries. Numbers of cases reported were totally inaccurate. A person testing positive twice for corona were reported as two cases.

So, we had these two opposing groups and two opposing ideas of what was going on and what should be done during the pandemic between politicians, state officials, scientists, and citizens and physicians.

Overall, the protestors believed that until the cave dwellers developed the courage to stand up for themselves, they would remain chained to the cave living in misery, fear, anger, and hopelessness. And they will never see the daylight outside the cave.

## Jack Was Horrified When the Hypocrisy Was Revealed

They started to see the hypocrisy of some politician lunatics. They saw Obama out golfing while his wife Michelle was on TV telling everyone to stay home. Also, Governor Cuomo's brother who claimed he had corona told all he was quarantined in his basement only to be spotted outside jogging on the sidewalk with no mask when everyone else was forced to stay in their homes.

Furthermore, one governor was on TV mandating the shut down on boating for Memorial Day and her husband was at the marina insisting his boat be retrieved so he could go boating. When the marina employee said no its closed, he said I'm the governor's wife does make a difference? Another governor was pontificating on TV how no one could go outside, only to find his wife out in the open enjoying the fresh air and sunlight. Still another governor was on TV and said everyone in his state must wear a mask while outside and must observe the social distancing guidelines. The next day that governor is on the beach taking a selfie with a woman on the beach. He had no mask on, with his arm around the woman for the picture. Absolutely no social distancing or mask wearing was being observed. Indeed, all these officials when confronted became defensive and had a *"**How dare you question my actions.**"*

## Jack was even More Horrified When the Corruption in NHI, CDC and FDA Was Revealed

It was unraveling that the top epidemiologist/physician on national committees making recommendations to the President was pushing the hysteria and propaganda about hydroxychloroquine. They had relationships with groups invested in other competitive medications. If hydroxychloroquine was used and found to be successful the scientists with patents for other medications stood to lose millions of dollars. Every attempt was made to try to discredit the hydroxychloroquine's positive effects when used early.

Further, efforts were made to discredit the scientists whose research and testimony on how well hydroxychloroquine worked. They were being discredited by the patented scientists and by the media. The media did the discrediting for the corrupt scientists in newspaper articles, television and social media.

Finally, it was revealed over time that these same epidemiologist and physicians were also involved in supporting the viral studies in China with taxpayer's money and had big stakes in the vaccine that was being developed.

Moreover, the scientists who were providing leadership to the country on what citizens should and should not do during the pandemic were using inaccurate, faulty fraudulent data. The numbers of cases were inflated to instill fear to keep the lock downs in place.

Sadly, they were also, stifling opposing scientists' research papers from being published in refereed medical journals. They were hell bent on discrediting the researchers' whose study disputed the scientists who had patents and or relationships with groups working on competitive medications.

The scientists once on a pedestal placed there by the media became defensive if they were challenged in any way were starting to lose their credibility.

Emerging now were frontline practicing emergency room and general practitioner physicians who saw firsthand the positive effects of the hydroxychloroquine were being discredited by the media. The same physicians were pressured to list all deaths as corona to make the rates look higher than they were. Their Y-tube presentations of the facts dispelling the corrupt scientist's recommendations were taken down from Y-tube. Social media was in cahoots with perpetuating the propaganda. Over time, the hypocrisy and corruption were becoming very apparent to even the progressive ideologues.

Trumps rating were rising especially among the independents and the last-ditch effort to defeat Trump by the democrats was failing dramatically. The economy was booming to the disappointment of the Anti Trumpers.

Jack is not a political person, but what he saw going on disturbed him greatly.

## All of the Confusion Led to Citizens Coming Out of the Cave in Droves

People were coming out of the cave in droves. The media's attempt to keep people at home shivering with fear failed. Specifically, restaurants, retail stores, beaches, parks, hiking trails, hair salons, gyms, and other businesses were opening to the public. Schools and colleges were resuming classes. Moreover, people were attending church services, sports events were resuming, concerts were being held, and drive-in movies were opened. Citizens however were still wearing mask and observing the social distance guidelines. But they were getting their lives back to some degree of normalcy.

Thankfully, the crushed economy was coming back slowly, unemployment rate was dropping. Families were able to put food on the table. Hospitals resumed the elective surgeries so people who could walk with severe knee bone on bone conditions and could once again get their total knee replacements. Dentists were now able to see patients for dental care. Patients were able to resume their cancer treatments. Life in America was coming back again.

However, people 65 and older came back slower and at this point. Restrictions were still in place for visitors in nursing homes, assisted care facilities and senior home complexes. These restrictions will probably be in place till there is a vaccine to protect the elderly.

In fact, it was reported that even though lock down restrictions were still in place in some states the citizens were rebelling. The nation was coming out of the cave in big time. The citizens started filing lawsuits because their rights were being trampled on. They were defying the political officials who executed the orders. In some states the police were ruthless in arresting the rebelling citizens and other states police were supporting the citizens and refused to arrest the citizens for violating the lock down law. Inconsistencies were seen across the entire nation.

Nevertheless, the economy was pulling out of the tank, unemployment was dropping. The nation was on the road to slow recovery, but a recovery non the less. As citizens were resurrected from their cave Jack reflected on how happy he was that his wife got the corona before this medication controversy occurred. He shutters at the thought that his wife may have gotten caught into this political firestorm and denied the hydroxychloroquine. If she got caught in that political storm, he said she may have ended up in the hospital on a ventilator and may not still be here with him.

## Jacks Goals to Lift Ann's Spirits with All the Chaos Going On

With all the disruption going on Jack was pleased with himself for using his time wisely during lock down. He is now anxious to discuss his plans for connecting his wife with the special needs' children once again with the activity director at the home with online technology.

Specifically, his goal is to lift Ann's spirits. He wants to eradicate her defeated attitude and mentality that took a stronghold on her when the volunteers were restricted. He wanted her to enlarge her vision to see that she was doing something meaningful and achieving significance once again. He wanted her to feel talented and valued with a sense of purpose.

In the meantime, he is relentless in trying to help Ann come out of the cave now. All his efforts are now directed at achieving this goal. He will not give up till this is achieved. He is one extraordinary man. His wife is one fortunate woman to have a husband that advocates for her in every way humanly possible. Jack reflected on what lessons he learned through this total chaos.

*11*

———∽∽———

# Key Lessons for America from the Pandemic

**Despite our differences** in religion, race or social standings we are all one, and the COVID-19 virus is proving that because it's not discriminating in the people. It's infecting every race, gender, sexual orientation or any divisions we have among ourselves as humans. And the way the virus spread from one country all throughout the world shows how we have a lot of things that connect and unite us that we can use to our advantage and definitely no man is an island

The corona virus is a mega-pandemic, if ever there was one. No other outbreak, affected people in as many countries as this one has. Nothing in Jack's lifetime (and he's 77 now) has ever caused the world to shut down. Every country that has tried to follow a different path, calibrated or otherwise, has discovered that a shutdown is inevitable. The impact was so swift and widespread that we were forced to learn new lessons and rediscover the value of some old ones much to our chagrin. Here are lessons that were discovered or learned. The list is by no means exhaustive, but provides food for thought.

## Positive Lessons Learned

**Gratefulness:** The people became profoundly grateful for their family, friends, and their freedoms. They realized how little they need, how much they have and how important human connection is to their emotional well-being. They were grateful for the many things they took for granted, such as the great outdoors with its rays of sun and cool, soothing breezes. They were grateful for their rights, and freedoms protected by the constitution as they got a taste for what it's like to live in a fascist socialistic country.

The lesson here is practicing gratitude and being grateful for the good things is our lives makes us happier and healthier.

**Look for The Positive:** Covid-19 incident taught us in every situation, no matter how negative it is, you can always find a spark of light. And this is also the case here. Being reminded to be grateful for what you have, being able to slow down, experiencing joy from sharing with the ones you love. Life is what you make of it. If you solely focus on the negative, that's all you'll ever see. But if you care to look beyond that, you'll find the golden nuggets hidden away in the mud.

The lesson here is that being positive is a choice one makes. Having a positive outlook means that you can look past those troubles and see things in a new way with positive light.

**American Spirit:** The crisis presented a rare opportunity to share our American identity and to celebrate our commonality as persons. Closed borders and travel bans, quarantine, shortage of food supply, food lines, scary news, and much fear was created among the people at all levels. Viruses don't care about our status, money, or fame, spreading from state officials to famous actors. We are all one.

The crisis revealed our weaknesses, but illuminated the profound American spirit of kindness, and generosity as Americans that we are capable of during an acute crisis. During times of physical disconnection, staying emotionally connected is a true blessing. Unity, collaboration, giving, support, community, service, compassion, inclusion, empathy, collaboration—such human values have never been so essential they were during the corona crisis.

The lesson here is that the American Spirit, is what made us great, and what makes us great to this day. The American Sprit can be seen, clearly, during times of national or regional crisis, or in our daily affairs, when Americans are generous, working for the common good, seeking progress during times of crisis.

**Society has a Heart:** The shutdown has, once again, shown us that society has a heart. We have seen individuals rise to the occasion and help elders take care of their daily needs, , organizations came forward to manufacture personal protective equipment, provide meals from factory kitchens, and administration opened up public buildings to provide space for those who need shelter or isolation. Central banks have brought in massive policy measures to help tide over the crisis and governments have provided the weaker sections of society with cash and food.

The lesson here is instances of doing good during this crisis are too numerous to enumerate comprehensively, but together they have re-established that society has a heart.

**Our Health Care Heroes:** Our front-line workers who put themselves in harm's way to take care of the people struck with the virus was extraordinary. Our hearts go out to all of them nurses, doctors, nursing assistants, respiratory therapists, blood and laboratory technicians, maintenance staff, housekeeping staff, dieticians, and all other interdisciplinary staff were our true heroes during this crisis.

The lesson here is that our health care workers often overlooked in society kept our society functioning while exposing themselves in harm's way. Their dedication, hard work and commitment never waned and were our true heroes during this pandemic.

**Non-Health Care Heroes were Revealed:** Our truck drivers, farmers, grocery store employees, shoppers, delivery employees, mail persons all put themselves in harm's way to help the cause. They are commended for their significant contributions and we will be eternally grateful to them for steeping up to the plate.

The lesson here is that these front-line workers are totally overlooked for their significant contributions to society. They too exposed themselves in harm's way were also keeping our nation going.

**Washing Hands Actually Work** This might sound ridiculous, but before the pandemic, most people might not have known that soap actually destroys certain kinds of viruses and bacteria. Nor did many know how to properly wash their hands. Now, having done a lot of reading on the subject, most people can probably explain in great detail why soap can obliterate microorganisms' outer membranes, including the coronavirus and why vigorous 20 second hand washing is critical. We'll probably wash our hands a lot more frequently after this is "over.

The lesson here is staying sudsy for at least 20 seconds frequently is now part of our daily routine.

**Faith:** Lock down orders, shortage of food supply, unemployment, terrifying news about the virus, and much fear brought to light how powerful hope and faith is for coping and getting through the crisis. Faith in facing the challenging times of crisis came to light in an extraordinary way. We learned that our faith allowed us to see opportunities where others see obstacles. Our faith allowed us to send encouraging words and help others where needed. Our faith caused us to kneel and pray for strength, direction, and peace. Our faith reminded us of the many obstacles that we have already overcome. Our faith sustained us and kept a grounded focus.

The lesson here is that for many God's spirit stirred up courage and strength, consolations, inspirations, and tranquility to face the uncertainty of the pandemic. It helped people to trust in the storm and helped them get through difficult times. It significantly quelled the overwhelming fear brought on by the unknown course of the virus.

**We Really Don't Need Much to Live:** We have lived through a lockdown. The availability of food, water, shelter, communication, medicines, education, entertainment on television and the internet has kept us going. The lockdown has forced us to ask what we really need to live reasonably well. And the answer in most cases is – not too much. While physiological and security needs have been paramount, many have found ways to learn new skills or do things they have always wanted to do, but couldn't make time for. Families and friends have engaged over video calls and many have "met" members of their family more often during the lockdown than they otherwise do! Despite the lockdown we have discovered that we can satisfy all needs in Maslow's hierarchy. Many have learnt what really matters to them.

The lesson here is that we all learned what really matters to us.

## Disappointing Lessons Learned

**China Dependency:** This crisis has revealed the complete dependency we have on China for the manufacturing of our medications, medical supplies, and food chain. Immediate steps need to be taken to bring the manufacturing of these items back to America. It brought to light how China has killed our dogs with deadly dog food, have given us ply board with asbestos, fish and meat with toxic substances in it and children's toys with leaded paint.

And during the pandemic they sent medical equipment to other countries masks and protective gear that was totally defective. God only knows what's in our medications and food. No more dependency on China. Tough sanctions must be placed on China for stealing intellectual property, military secrets, and electronic inventions. Efforts on their part are now active in trying to steal the vaccine findings from the

US and other countries to get a monopoly on the worldwide vaccine. The US must bring our manufacturing back home to prevent our dependency on an enemy country.

The lesson here is to never allow other nations to control our vital national assets.

**Rampant Nefarious Conflicts of Interest/ Corruption Internationally:** International World Health Organization (WHO): The WHO supposedly the group that guides the world on health issues was massively a corrupt organization. The WHO leader was bribed to support the China propaganda that corona could not spread to humans and that it was safe to keep the borders open that contributed significantly to the spread of corona worldwide.

The lesson learned is that WHO is a political corrupt body needs to be abolished, defunded, or restructured in a major way.

## National Corruption in US Government Health Organizations:

**National Institute of Health (NHI):** We learned that the NHI has no checks and balances to overlook their funding support. This could lead to potential massive fraud and corruption. Especially when one considers the large amount of money under the control of one entity. The Director National Institute of Allergy used over three million dollars taxpayers' money to support corona virus studies in death labs in China, knowing full well their safety practices were far below standards and that the research was extremely dangerous.

Despite the recommendations from scientists about their concerns related to the unsafe lab conditions, he went forward with the monetary support to China. One questions why taxpayer's money is being used to study corona virus in China. Also, one questions do the scientists that have patents or special interests to potential vaccines to cure the virus or treat the virus making substantial money should there be an outbreak.

Amazingly, the Bayh-Dole Act allows scientist to patent their work and is a huge conflict of interest and potential set up for massive corruption. Scientists have patents for drugs and vaccines and stands to make millions if their patented drugs and vaccines that are used to treat diseases. Thus, this presents the potential squeezing out other promising drugs competing with their patents. A huge unethical conflict of interest.

The Director National Institute of Allergy is connected to the Gates foundation. He supports the vaccine investments and efforts made by George Soros and Bill Gates. This support comes with a 100-million-dollar pledge from Gates Foundation to NHI. One has to question is this why he would not support the hydroxychloroquine medication used by physicians around the world to successfully treat the corona virus. Could it be that if it were revealed that the hydroxychloroquine drug worked there would be no need to have vaccine or no need for other medications that the Director was supporting. It is believed by many that Hydroxychloroquine was a threat to the Director of NHI if it indeed worked well in treating corona. He would stand to lose the 100-million-dollar pledge to NHI from the Gate's foundation.

It is believed by many that Hydroxychloroquine was a major threat to the vaccine investments of Gates and Soros. The 100 million that Gates pledged to give to NHI could be used in any fashion Director National Institute of Allergy wanted with no accountability or checks and balances at all. This is a huge potential fertile area that could result in corruption. It could potentially lead to embezzlement, money laundering and bribes that would benefit those in charge of using the Gates' million-dollar pledges. It is believed that the NHI has been infected with money and politics.

Indeed, the NHI has too much power and has too many conflicts of interest and potential corruption within the organization that lead to nefarious actions and personal payoffs from various organizations.

The lesson learned is that this government agency NHI needs to be restructured with checks and balances over seeing their functions, and their monetary donations. Moreover, the Bayh-Dole Act needs to be abolished to prevent corruption within the agency.

**The Center of Disease Control {CDC}:** The CDC was exposed for their horrific shortcomings in their operations. This critical governmental agency was miserably incompetent in its mission. The CDC was negligently sluggish. Instead of getting diagnostic testing in place they were more interested in protecting their turf then acting with urgency and with a sense of emergency. It acted as a lazy tortoise. Their initial testing kit was flawed. If the testing kits were handled in a proper fashion the scope of death and destruction would have been significantly less.

The CDC over diagnosed the number of corona cases purposely it is believed by many to instill fear in the citizens and to use as data to continue lockdown restrictions that supported the NHI ideology and globalists goals.

Their internal acts and procedures changed every five minutes confusing health care workers, nursing homes, hospitals, and citizens. The information they put out was inaccurate which contributed to death and destruction. The CDC obtuseness and incompetence goes far beyond misery and death. It will have political, diplomatic, and economic consequences as well.

The lesson learned is that the CDC needs new leadership to provide competent, timely accurate responses to emergencies.

**The Federal Food and Drug Administration (FDA):** The systematic corruption of the FDA was exposed during the pandemic. It was learned that past practices were unethical. Scientists received retaliation if they did not sign off on unsafe drugs. Pressure was placed on scientists to approve unsafe drugs from top officials that were tied to big business and Pharmaceutical companies. These top officials in bed with pharmaceutical companies were receiving handsome monetary rewards. Top officials fraudulently withheld information on the bad effects due to their connections with big pharm companies.

Conversely, scientists were discrediting drugs like hydroxychloroquine because there was no money to be made with this drug for big pharm. Finally, under pressure they came out with approval to use hydroxychloroquine for compassionate use, but recommended it only be given in a hospital under the supervision of a physician. This resulted in patients with corona being placed in a hospital and being given the drug too late after the cytokine inflammation storm set in when it was no longer effective. These nefarious activities were despicable and exposed before the eyes of the nation.

If hydroxychloroquine were given to the patient by their primary care physician, the patient would have received it right away when it was most effective and could have stayed at home to recuperate not taking up a hospital bed. This organization is corrupt, and their activities are disgraceful. They sell out patients to line their pockets with big pharm money.

The lesson learned is that Medicine has been infected with money and politics. There needs to be a law passed preventing scientist from connecting with big pharm and big foundations to receive big money.

**CORRUPTION IN US UNIVERSITIES:**

University researchers doing research with taxpayers' money and are also being paid by China. This is a creating a fertile area for huge conflict of interest and massive corruption. Some professors at our prestigious universities across the country are engaged in unethical, conflicts of interest and potential corruption. Our university professors are receiving huge sums of money for endowed chairs and research efforts from China that all seems genuinely nice and legal on the surface. But the payoff is resulting in the Chinese stealing our intellectual property, research findings and innovations.

Correspondingly, the professors turned a blind eye to China's corruption, stealing of research findings and intellectual property, because of the money they were lining their pockets with, money from China. Professors with no checks and balances for accountability for the donations are creating a fertile are for potential fraud in areas of embezzlement and money laundering. Sadly, universities have been infected with money and politics also.

In fact, it finally came out that two Harvard Professors published fraudulent studies discrediting the effectiveness of hydroxychloroquine. These studies were published in a well-respected Medical Journal. When the deceit and fraudulent data was discovered the articles had to be retracted for outright fraud. One must wonder what pay off the two crooked professors received for engaging in this skullduggery. And to think national policy was being formulated on these two fake studies. Disgraceful and scary.

The lesson here is there needs to be more checks and balances when universities receive funding from foreign countries for initiatives that seem on the surface to be benign such as endowed chairs and research funding.

**Corruption among our Politicians:**

Our own politicians have sold out our country to China and other countries to line their pockets with money by giving away all our manufacturing and vital resources like uranium. This corruption has tanked our economy and has contributed to unemployment of our citizens and has crushed the middleclass. It was revealed that politicians were selling access to foreign operatives to act on their behalf when foreign policy was made and not on behalf of America.

The lesson here is more oversight for politicians receiving donations to foundations, lecture honorariums, hidden donations to campaigns and sharing of vital national resources with foreign countries.

### Corruption Among Mainstream Media:

The corruption of our mainstream media is shameful. The propaganda lies they hit the citizens with every day to support their ideology is shameful and dishonorable. Their continuous 24/7 doom and gloom reports instilling fear supported all three of the corrupt National Health Care Governmental Agencies. One must wonder where their payoff and bribes are coming from.

The lesson here is that the media is not a friend of the people and are using lies and propaganda to support and brainwash citizens to supporting their political ideologies. The media is an extension of the liberal left, hellbent on taking away our freedoms, taking down America, withholding the truth, and pushing socialistic ideals. Journalistic goals have given way to a public relations role. True Journalism is dead in America.

### Abuse of Human Rights:

Generally, restrictions on personal liberties must be reasonable and necessary and made in good faith for the preservation of public health, safety order. The government cannot arbitrarily restrict liberties that don't have a legitimate purpose.

But during the pandemic personal liberties were violated by power hungry politicians with a specific ideology that crushed the constitution and the economy and the citizens spirits. Government officials trampled on the citizens right in the name of protecting the health of the population. The coronavirus pandemic has taken a huge toll on the civil liberties Americans hold dear.

Can't go to church? Can't buy a gun? Can't go to the beach? Can't go out in your yard, can't get a haircut, can't go out in your boat, can't visit grandma. Americans are told to stay home. Some states try to block residents of other states from entering their state.

One could go into Walmart, Sam's Club, and BJ's because they were considered essential to buy paint ,plant seed, fabric, eye glasses, ice cream and meat, but **could not** go to an eye glass store to buy glasses, or a paint store to buy paint, or to an ice cream store to buy ice cream or a fabric store to buy fabric or a nursery to buy plant seed or to a butcher shop to buy meat. These places were not considered essential thus they were all shut down.

Ironically, one could buy alcohol, and marijuana because they were essential services, but could not go to an AA meeting or have a funeral. One could get an abortion because it was declared essential, but citizens could not get a total knee replacement for severe pain or have a stress test for cardiac assessment or have a colonoscopy to screen for cancer.

Indeed, these restrictions imposed in many states have not just made life difficult – they have infringed upon the most basic rights guaranteed under the US Constitution. Many of the violations of rights were political in nature and were not based on science or data. They were arbitrarily ordered and seen as draconian restrictions of citizens basic constitutional rights. The officials were emotionally bullying citizens who wanted to open their business', go to church, buy guns, have elective surgery performed, engage in protests against the lock downs. But BLM, a group hijacked by a Marxist trained operative and Antifa could protest, because this was done in the name of social justice. The mayors and governors of some states laid guilt trips on the citizens for not caring about the spread of the virus, labeling them irresponsible, selfish, racist, and Nazis. But not a word was said to control the violent protests by BLM and Antifa.

### Amendments that were Violated During Pandemic:

Sadly, many constitutional amendments were violated without scientific evidence to support the lock down. Specifically, below are a list of amendments that were violated

**The First Amendment was violated:** First Amendment freedoms of speech and free association, with restraints on the freedom of religion were imposed on the people. Some groups were denied protest permits and were arrested if they protested. Other groups in the same city with no protest permits were allowed to protest with no arrests. The incosistencies on who could protest and who could not were disgraceful. People were arrested for attending church in an open lot in their cars while listening to the preacher on a large movie like screen. Physicians speaking out on Y tube about the injustices being perpetrated were shut down. Peoples Twitter and Facebook accounts were shut down if they spoke out against the left-wing ideology in Democratic run states.

The lesson here is that laws need to be in place to allow prosecution of Governors, Mayors and social media tech companies who violate freedom of speech.

**The Second Amendment was violated:** Mayors declared the right to ban gun sales. Governments declared background-check personnel were not permitted to process a background check, delaying gun sales indefinitely, and other governments simply shut down all gun sales businesses entirely. This happens while governments release inmates into the streets, and, at the same time, issue no-arrest and no-detention orders from a wide range of criminals. Those who want to defend themselves, give themselves a sense of personal protection that comes with gun ownership for many, as the Second Amendment safeguards went out the window. Again, liquor and marijuana were declared essential, but buying a gun was non-essential and could not be bought.

The lesson here is to pass laws to prevent Mayors and Governors from using the pandemic as an excuse to foster their ideologies and trample on the constitution.

**The Fourth Amendment was violated:** Few protections are more American than the right to privacy against coerced, compelled, secretive, subversive invasion. The government operates like a virus in a case of a pandemic panic, infecting our minds and bodies, monitoring speech, association, and movement, with tools of surveillance unthought-of to the founders. Coordinating with private companies (unrestrained by the Fourth Amendment. This is why the NSA uses them to gather all your emails, conversations, texts, and internet searches, at the first stage?), governments used the panic about the pandemic, a panic the government itself stoked with aid of a compliant, complicit press, to waive your medical privacy and invade your personal privacy, looking for tools to monitor your every movement, associations, activities, and behavior. The watching eye in the sky can now be the Alexa in your home, the camera on your computer, and the phone in your hand. Privacy is ended. The US Constitution is quarantined.

The lesson here is that Big Tech and NSA must be reined in to prevent the surveillance, subversive invasion of our privacy and invade our medical and personal privacy.

**The Fifth Amendment was violated:** The protection for our right to make a living arises from the Fifth Amendment right to property without deprivation by due process of law, and the obligation for the government to compensate any such takings. Yet, governments across America did just that to millions of businesses, workers, and property owners, stripping them of their ability to make a living, or even to engage in a free market of commerce, by shutdown orders, curfews, and stay-at-home orders. The political and professional class ensconced in its work-from-home environs fails to appreciate the hardship this imposes on working people.

The lesson learned is that the people shouldn't be afraid of their government. Governments should be afraid of their people. Only when an awake public asserts their human liberties to protest the loss of their liberties will, then, governments quit using public health crises to seize power that does not belong to them.

## Shameless, Flagrant Hypocrisy Among our Government Officials Exposed:

We learned how hypocritical our elected officials are in the face of a national crisis. The rules are for everyone else but them. They showed their true colors and how they view their constituents with total contempt. Elected politicians, mayors and governors went out to the gym, the park, played golf, ate in restaurants without observing social distancing or wearing masks and had hair cuts in salons, but the common citizens were threatened with arrest if they did the same.

The lesson is that we need to hold our politicians accountable for following the same rules and executive orders as the common citizen must follow.

## Lack of Preparation for Pandemic Emergencies:

The National stockpile of medical equipment was woefully lacking. The nation was totally unprepared for a viral pandemic. There was no reserve of personal protective equipment for health care worker. Masks, gowns, ventilators were sorely lacking. Testing equipment took forever to obtain. Guidelines were inaccurate. Our three health care government agencies' NHI, CDC, NHI were slow to respond and proved to be totally incompetent, ideology driven, and unethical.

The lesson learned is that a group comprised of frontline doctors and healthcare workers must develop a plan of action for pandemics and not the dinosaur governmental bureaucrats from CDC, NHI and FDA sitting in an office with no frontline experience in caring for patients.

## Nursing Home Scandal in New York:

Governor Andrew Cuomo of New York ordered nursing homes in the Empire State to accept patients carrying the coronavirus — bringing carriers of the potentially deadly organism into proximity with those most vulnerable to being killed by it. New York State barred people from visiting their loved ones in nursing homes, while simultaneously forcing infected patients into the same places.

When nursing home residents with corona were discharged from the hospital because they no longer required nursing care, but still able to shed the virus were forced back into the nursing home killing 5,000 seniors. Governor Cuomo was informed that the nursing homes were not set up to handle patients in isolation and they also were short on personal protective equipment putting all the staff at risk also. His flippant comment was if you're operating a nursing home you need to know how to manage residents with corona. His condescension and arrogance were deplorable.

In fact, the Javits Center set up to care for patients with corona and the Navy ship set up to handle patients with corona were never utilized by Cuomo. The beds sat empty. It was disgraceful that he didn't lift a finger to help and protect our elderly. It was a shameful policy Cuomo put into place with no feeling of remorse. The elderly was expendable, the staff were looked down upon and the nursing homes, pleas for help ignored in an arrogant fashion. The nursing home cries for help fell on deaf ears. He may as well have put a sign up saying: **"Elderly Lives Don't Matter".**

Our most vulnerable nursing home residents were neglected. Nursing Home protection keeping elderly Americans safe from COVID-19 should be a #1 priority during the pandemic, because they're at the highest risk of contracting the virus and dying from its virulent course.

Among these older people, the most vulnerable are the 1.5 million people who live in nursing homes. But this group- who are too sick to care for themselves- have largely been ignored by government and health officials.

The lesson learned here was to pour a large portion of the resources and attention into nursing homes and assisted care facilities as they did in Florida to protect the most vulnerable.

## Lack of Strategies to Manage Painful Isolation Nursing Homes:

America was in the depths of a public health crisis when the coronavirus outbreak hit: one of social isolation and loneliness. Nursing homes restricted family and volunteer visits to prevent the spread of the virus throughout the home like a wildfire. But it resulted in extreme emotional stress, loneliness, and anxiety among the residents. Nursing homes were totally unprepared to manage this problem.

In some cases, this loneliness experienced by the residents was worse than the virus itself. Many residents starting showing signs of **failure to thrive** not from corona, but sheer isolation.

Every nursing home should consider an activity staff member as an essential employee who develops a plan with strategies to overcome the isolation imposed by visiting restrictions.

Some examples to consider in the future are Videoconferencing applications to allow residents to visit with family members, like FaceTime, Skype, and Google Hangouts. These enable the elderly to not only communicate with friends and family, but see their familiar faces. The nursing home should consider an activity person as essential to ensure the technology devices are clean and can assist the resident who are technologically incompetent in using the technology.

Letters and cards were restricted to enter the home. The home should have an approved means to accept letters or cards for lonely residents. Everyone enjoys getting "good" mail from the post office, and it's even more true at a nursing home. The letters and cards and envelops can be sprayed with a disinfecting spray (e.g., Lysol),

Virtual social events could be utilized, but would require some internal technical setup on the part of the nursing home. Many of the activities that seniors enjoy can be done with social distancing through technology. With a combination of webcams and videoconferencing applications (and a skilled host), the home can connect residents for games like bingo, trivia, and karaoke. This type of setup is used in business all the time, and it doesn't require a ton of money or technical sophistication to bring a sense of fun, community, and normalcy to the elderly loved ones you know.

Virtual pets since service dogs were not permitted in the home during the pandemic such as furry dogs that move and wag their tail could be given to each resident to hug and pet. It would bring comfort to those who are animal lovers.

The lesson to learn is the need to plan for activities and interaction to overcome and prevent social isolation within the nursing home during a crisis to prevent failure to thrive.

## Closing Remarks

Indeed, there could be entire books written on the lessons learned, some that were not even mentioned such as educational strategies to teach children at home, focusing on fact not fiction, more detailed strategies for eliminating corruption in medicine and national healthcare governmental agencies, involving front line nurses and physicians in forecasting what resources are needed to care for the patients, how to be more effective in the testing process, identifying more effective models for forecasting predictions, how to balance safety while protecting human rights, how to put political differences aside to manage the pandemic appropriately. For sure, the list goes on and on and could fill an entire volume of books. But the above lists are just a few lessons learned both positive and negative from the pandemic that Jack Long lived through and learned.

## 12

## ANN IS NOW IN HEAVEN

**ANN RECOVERED COMPLETELY** from the corona virus. No coughing, congestion, fever, cytokine storm. She was progressing very well from the corona virus now for six weeks.

However, after six weeks, Jack received a call from the nursing home saying Ann is not eating well and is not drinking enough fluids. He begged them to find some food she liked to eat. He explained she was a fussy eater. When Jack was able to visit if she didn't eat, he'd go in the kitchen and round up something she'd like so she would eat. He's now feeling awful. He feels if he were able to visit, he could get her to eat. They had to start intravenous fluids.

Truly, her turn for the worse had nothing to do with the corona. She was showing signs of failure to thrive. With no visits from Jack, her therapy dog or her favorite volunteers, and not being allowed to visit her favorite resident friend she was showing signs that she has lost her will to live. It is believed that she was on the verge of giving up wanting to die. Wanting to join her parents in heaven. She was ready to move on to her next journey. And she was making a conscious decision to do that. Jack is heartbroken. Sad beyond words.

Considering this, each day he checks with the nursing home to see how she is doing. He and his son set up more frequent conference calls to cheer her up. These calls were successful in helping to restore her will to live. Even though she was suffering from severe isolation and loneliness, the conference calls helped to life her spirits.

To Jack's delight he was able to do a window visit with Ann on Mother's Day. Jack came to the home at a specified time and stood outside the window to see Ann. He was able to talk to her through the window and Ann was able to hear him. He had difficulty hearing Ann. The nurse interpreted what she said to Jack. Finally, they spoke on the phone while they saw each other through the window.

For the purpose of cheering her up he brought a cardboard box with Happy Mother's Day written on it along with the names of all her friends who missed her. He lifted the box up so she could read it through the window. Additionally, he had a card he was able to share with her that told her he loved her. It also said he missed her, and he wanted her to stay strong and continue to eat and drink water.

Unbelievably, this window visit was the first time Ann and Jack saw each other in three months. It was a heart wrenching visit for Jack, and Ann. The nurses all crying with joy.

Disappointingly, this visit did not go well with Ann. The visit did not cheer Ann as expected. She was suffering from severe social isolation and she was sad to say the least. She cried the entire time not from joy, but from sadness. Jack said "Ann why are you crying? You're doing so well. People are dying all over and you're doing fine." She replied "I'm going to die next and I'm not going to eat." This of course was not what Jack expected. He was sad to say the least. With her continued crying and no conversation Jack eventually said goodbye to Ann. He told he loved her and then left.

Although, Ann recovered from corona by a miracle, the social isolation imposed by the nursing home visitation restrictions was impacting significantly on Ann. She missed her daily visits with her husband, her favorite volunteers, the other residents, her friends, and her therapy dog visit. All these visits came a screeching halt. She missed the festive celebrations the nursing home had for holidays, birthdays, and anniversaries. She was in solitary confinement in isolation still. The only interaction she had was with a different nurse each day who came in to give her nursing care. Her only view from the bed was the ceiling and the four walls in the room.

On the negative side, Jack received a call several days later from the home saying Ann was declining significantly. She was not eating or drinking. And was going into a slump. Her son called immediately and told her to start eating and drinking. They scheduled a second window visit for Jack to see if he could cheer her up. The second window visit went much better. Jack and his son were happy that things were on the upward swing for Ann. She was eating better and trying hard to interact in a more enthusiastic manner.

However, this upward swing didn't last long. Another call several days later revealed Ann had nothing to eat for breakfast lunch or dinner. She was in excruciating pain. They started Ann on morphine. Jack had a third window visit scheduled for the next day. He was preparing himself and his son for the worst. This third visit was not satisfying for Jack. Ann was not able to respond since she was receiving intravenous morphine.

Indeed, the nursing home visitation restrictions created social isolation in the nursing home. Ann not seeing her husband twice a day for over four months took a major toll on her spirits. She had nothing to do when she woke up, nothing to look forward to, and no holiday celebrations to participate in. This impacted on her will to go on. Since she was a very social person, she needed personal interaction to survive. She was in an isolation wing of the home and saw no one all day except for the nurse who came in to provide nursing care.

Clearly, social isolation is a serious health risk. Studies of elderly people and social isolation concluded that those without adequate social interaction were twice as likely to die prematurely.

Importantly, new research suggests the effects of social isolation, namely anxiety, aggression, and memory impairment result from altered levels of an enzyme that controls production of a brain hormone.

Furthermore, social isolation can affect your mental and emotional health as well as your physical well-being. Without enough social interaction, you may be at risk of emotional, mental, and physical decline. Social isolation can also get in the way of everyday functioning. In fact, it can throw off sleep patterns, disrupt focus, decrease appetite, and affect both logical and verbal reasoning.

**UNDOUBTEDLY, ALL THESE EFFECTS WERE MANIFESTED IN ANN TO THE POINT WHERE SHE LOST HER WILL TO LIVE.**

Human beings are social creatures. Our connection to others enables us to survive and thrive. Yet, as we age, many of us are alone it leaves us vulnerable to social isolation and loneliness—and related health problems such as cognitive decline, depression, and heart disease.

Clearly, the misery and suffering Ann experienced being in isolation was alarming. "Loneliness acts as a fertilizer for other diseases," as stated by Dr. Steve Cole, Director of the Social Genomics Core Laboratory at the University of California, Los Angeles. According to Dr. Cole, the biology of loneliness can accelerate the buildup of plaque in arteries, help cancer cells grow and spread, and promote inflammation in the brain leading to Alzheimer's disease. Loneliness promotes several different types of wear and tear on the body.

At this time, Jack in retrospect wonders if the breast and ovarian cancer Ann refused treatments for many years ago may have raised its ugly head again. He wondered if the cancer was causing her pain that they had to give her morphine for.

Obviously, Jack is now incredibly sad knowing he's going to lose his wife forever. He is reminiscing on what a wonderful person Ann was, how kind she was to others, how much she did for the special needs children she worked with. Thoughts of his wife were flooded his mind in a constant manner.

First and foremost, Jack is now showing signs and symptoms of anticipatory grief that included: intense sorrow, pain, and rumination over the loss of a loved one. He focused on little else but his wife's death.

Specifically, anticipatory grief can be like grief after death, but is also unique in many ways. Grief before death often involves more anger, more loss of emotional control, and atypical grief responses. This may be related to the difficult place—the "in-between place" people find themselves in when a loved one is dying.

At this time, Jack remarked that he felt so mixed up inside, because he felt he kept failing in his attempt to find that tender balance between holding on to hope and letting go.

In particular, anticipatory grief provided Jack an opportunity for personal growth at the end of life, a way to find meaning and closure. For him, this period was also an opportunity to find closure, to reconcile differences, and to give and grant forgiveness.

At this time, he felt sadness and tearfulness. Sadness and tears tended to rise rapidly and often when he least expected. Even small things, such as a song or a sight may be a sudden and painful reminder that Ann was dying; almost as if it is again the first time, he's aware of his impending loss.

Likewise, he expressed he was afraid. Feelings of fear are common and include not only the fear of death, but fear about all the changes that will be associated with losing Ann.

Subsequently, he found himself in a heightened state of anxiety all the time. He was experiencing physical symptoms such as tremulousness, palpitations, and shaking. He was experiencing physical problems such as sleep difficulty and memory problems. His thinking was cloudy. His appetite was declining.

Moreover, his loneliness resulted in a strong desire to talk to someone—anyone—who might understand how he felt and listen without judgment. He needed to talk to prevent social withdrawal or emotional numbness to protect the pain in his heart. Jack found comfort in talking with his sister Ellen and his friend Mary. He called other friends who tried to comfort him.

In addition, Jack found himself visualizing what it will be like to have Ann gone. He visualized how he will carry on after her death. Many people feel guilty about these thoughts, but they are very normal and are part of accepting the inevitability of death.

Indeed, for Jack, the time prior to Ann's death was a time of great guilt—because Ann was suffering. He longed for her to be free of pain (and hence, die), but feared the moment that death will actually happen. It was thought that Jack was experiencing survivor guilt, a guilt that he will be able to continue on with his life, while Ann will not.

Additionally, he was overwhelmed with anger. Anger that Ann was so stubborn and would not consent to surgery for her breast and ovarian cancer a few years ago. Thoughts went through his mind that if only she agreed to treatment maybe she may have survived longer. He begged her to get treatment, but she adamantly declined treatment.

As it turned out the stomach pain, she was experiencing was the cancer. It spread throughout her system and was causing pain. It was believed that the prolonged painful social isolation helped the cancer cells to spread.

Indeed, this was a difficult time for him. He had a roller coaster of emotions, feelings, and physical manifestations.

Finally, he received the dreaded call from the nursing home telling Jack that Ann died. He was in shock. Although he expected her to pass it was a shock when the time actually came.

What's more, a part of him was relieved that she died peacefully with the angels who took her on her journey to heaven. And the other part of him was filled with sadness for his extraordinary loss.

Hence, for Ann it's over the last struggle in past, the strife, anxiety, pain, and turmoil of life is over. Henceforth, Ann's great life marked at every step will be remembered with fondness and love forever.

Certainly, Ann's passing fell heavy on the hearts of Jack and Jack Jr.

They took comfort when reflecting on what an extraordinary woman she was. She was a warm person who loved working with special needs children. She had a special knack of bonding with them that no one else could achieve. She was a brilliant accountant. She loved cruises, Virginia Beach, shopping, concerts, and travel. She led friends and family into a kinder, loving, more compassionate world. She was esteemed by all who knew her. The kindliness and tenderness of her heart was seen and felt by all came within her charmed circle of intimacy.

Positively, when people thought of Ann they thought of her warm heart, her desire to do nice things for others, her air of dignity, her joy of being around people and her generosity.

Indeed, she has left a void that no one can fill-laid forever at rest. When Jack sees the bright sun shining down or a bright star in the sky, he will think of Ann. She was his sunshine and his bright star.

Surely, she has left behind numerous memories that will never be forgotten. When someone you love becomes a memory they leave behind a treasure. Ann left many wonderful memories for her family and for all who knew and loved Ann.

Prior to Ann's stroke her life was filled with joy, hope, enthusiasm, courage, and love. Her life was a great one full packed with fun and adventure and was surrounded by a loving husband, and son, and other family members.

With Ann's passing her life lives on. She lives on in each one of her friends and family with her warm, loving spirit. The power of God has allowed Ann to resurrect her spirit within each of her family members and friends. She has given them restoration and hope to move forward.

Undeniably, there is certainly a special spot in heaven for Jack. There is a saying that says, "how you handle your tough times stays with you for a long time". Jack has handled his tough times time with grace, dignity, sacrifice, commitment. He put all his needs on the back burner to be by Ann's side every day taking care of her medical needs, offering comfort, support, love, and entertainment to keep her spirits up.

Without fail he has been there every single day for eight years twice a day visiting Ann rain, snow, sleet or shine he was there. Opening her milk carton, feeding her breakfast and lunch, making sure she got up out of the bed every day. He made sure she's in a comfortable position in the wheelchair, making sure she got her haircuts and showers, rubbing her legs when they hurt. He advocated for her in every way he could. He did everything humanly possible to care for Ann. He was the best husband any wife could hope for. He is an inspiration to all.

Thus, Jack now has the challenge of creating a life without Ann. Jack will make his life purposeful and infuse Ann's spirit in others. He will tap into Ann's pure gold and inoculate others with her warm, loving spirit to give strength to others in need, so they can lead an abundance of life as Ann did. In Ann's legacy Jack will bring hope, joy, and peace to others.

## 13

## Jack Faced with Creating a New Life

**With Ann's passing** Jack was faced with creating a new life for himself. He wasn't sure where he would end up living but he knew he wanted to move out of New York. New York became an unfriendly state for him to live in with its weather, taxes, and politics. It was sad for him because he was born and raised in New York and always enjoyed the state immensely.

Specifically, shoveling all that snow and mowing his lawn at age 77 and paying the high taxes with his modest financial situation became a hardship for him. His son who lives in San Diego had a spare room in his home and offered Jack the opportunity to live with him and his wife. The thoughts he tossed around in his mind were living with his son for six months. This would give him some quality time with his son and an opportunity to meet his friends and learn more about his sons thriving business. And for the remaining six months perhaps rent a small apartment in Georgia to live closer to his sister Ellen and her husband who he is so fond of. Living in Georgia for six months would allow him to go hunting, fishing, and go golfing with John. He could also partake in a great home cooked meal prepared by Ellen. Living in Georgia for six months would afford him the opportunity to meet their friends and perhaps meet new friends. This would make him incredibly happy and less lonely living half time in California and Georgia.

It was difficult for Jack to think of making any changes now being in such a profound state of grief. He had a hole is his heart which nothing could fill. He felt that everything was upside down and very confusing for him. Suddenly his life was moving in a new direction and he had no idea where he was going. He felt numb and some mornings when he woke up just surviving the day was all he could do.

Not surprisingly, it was like the light in his world went dark and he wondered if it would ever be rekindled. He felt completely disjointed and his perception of time was so different from everyone else's. He was now faced dealing with things he never dealt with before and this was anxiety provoking for him. He was feeling overwhelmed. He was so painfully lonely and cried at he thought of living the rest of his life alone and abandoned. He is terrified of living his life alone.

In fact, his life now was shattered into fragments, and he felt they could never be put back together again. He experienced anger for Ann leaving him and then was angered at himself for feeling that way. It took months before he stopped waking up in the morning getting ready to visit Ann then realizing she's no longer with him. There were times he couldn't wait to tell Ann a piece of news until he realized she's gone and never coming back. The sadness swept over him in waves. A song, a smell, a memory, picture, or a sight would hit him like a brick and he'd become overwhelmed with tears. He had nightmares and was not able to sleep. At 4PM in the afternoon he was so tired he fell asleep at the drop of a hat. He pretended he was OK with friends, but it was all an act. He was not OK.

Specifically, Jack had to learn how to overcome the painful loneliness and thoughts of how can he go on without Ann was a huge challenge for Jack. Likewise, had to learn how to deal with the anxiety of not having Ann in his life. Moreover, he had to learn how to overcome the guilt of surviving. Finding the energy to carry out activities of daily living was a monumental task. Jack had to learn how to make his life purposeful again. However, the biggest challenge of all for Jack was coping with the extreme loneliness.

Can you imagine what it is like to lose a spouse that you spent 56 years with, raising their son with, laughing and crying with and ultimately grew old with? Imagine how that feels.

He wondered if he'd ever be able to create a new life without Ann.

With the loss of Ann, he lost not only his partner, but the person who gave him stability and confidence. The person who made all of the major decisions giving him peace of mind and who shared in the outcome of their days in their lives.

To Jack's credit, with the help of friends who experienced recent loses also he over time learned he had to make a new life. He began to learn that he could survive the unimaginable. He took one step at a time, one day at a time. He learned the pain doesn't ever go away but it does get easier to bear. But he found it helpful to talk with friends and his sister Ellen about his feelings of loss.

In essence, as he started moving forward in creating a new life, he had a dream one night that he had a camper with his car towed behind it. He went to Georgia to visit his sister and her husband. Then he travelled to Florida to visit his friend Mary and her husband. As he traversed the country, he then went to Les Vegas to visit with one of his best friends and then on to California to visit with his son.

Uniquely, all his life he traveled from the northeast to the southeast exploring the White Mountains of New Hampshire to the beaches all along the east coast. On his numerous cruises he's explored all the Islands. But he's never been out west to see the Grand Canyon, Badlands, Yosemite National Park, Monument Valley or the famous Antelope Slot Canyon. He has set that as one of his goals to accomplish. Beyond that whatever he does he knows his new life will involve hunting, fishing, golfing, and volunteering at a homeless shelter.

As he continued to think about his future, he harkened back to the days when he went fishing with his friend Justin. They had such a good time laughing. Justin's humor was a bit crude at times, but Jack enjoyed it unlike others. He always had a new story to tell. Jack was an avid fisherman. He usually went on his one day off from work. He'd go early in the morning so he could get back to take Ann shopping since she did not drive. He and Justin would get in the car with coffee mug in hand and off they went. In about 45 minutes they arrived at their fishing spot. As Jack looked over the lake, he saw the sun coming up. It was beautiful and peaceful. He thought this is going to be a great day. The caffeine from the coffee kicked in and he was feeling good. Jack placed his large tackle box on the ground. He proudly opened his dazzling new tackle box. He marveled at the bright sun light coming down from the heavens. Jack must have had hundreds of dollars' worth of tackles and gear in his box.

Expertly, Jack reached for a specific lure, skillfully attached it to the end of the line and casted away. Justin reached for a cold beer and it was only 6AM and Jack passed since he had to drive Ann to the grocery store when he got back. One can see why this is so popular in the fishing paradise. After about ten minutes of casting they were pulling in some good size redfish. After about 90 minutes Jack looked in the cooler and it was already filled with fish. Now they changed their lure to catch a few speckled trout. Two hours later they were on their way home. To Jack's disappointment he always had to cut the fishing time down to get back to Ann.

Interestingly, the next morning, he was back on the job. He thought about the fishing trip the day before and a light bulb went on viewing the analogy to his fishing trips and his job. He knew his work evaluations and performance depended on how well the people he supervised carried out their responsibilities. Everything was dependent on how well he motivated and led his employees.

Expressly, as he went back to his thoughts on fishing, he realized how easy it was to catch exactly the kind of fish he wanted because he gave the fish what they wanted. And as supervisor he thought he was given his employees what they wanted. Or was he giving them the communication style, motivational style, and leadership style he thought was best. Suddenly, it dawned on him to get the results he wanted achieved he had to give the employees what they wanted. He recognized at that moment that he could enhance better results if he made some changes in his behaviors, so he added more lures in his tackle box to make his employees feel more valued and appreciated. One thing his employees admired about Jack was his patience. His one virtue of patience that served him well on the job he was proud of and he attributed his patience directly to his love of fishing.

Likewise, thoughts of his hunting days started to peculate from his subconscious. On his one day off he went to his hunting area during the season early in the morning before his wife even arose. He dressed in his warmest, lightest clothes to keep warm and to feel comfortable. He felt excitement and a mix of emotions. Sitting under a tree shivering from the cold and wondered how it would all pan out. Would it be a successful hunt, or would he come home empty handed.

Markedly, he learned about a successful hunt. It was more than its conclusion; it was about the journey and the lessons learned along the way. He loved the outdoors and felt an enormous respect for the wild. With his seven-day work week busy and stressful the hunting pulled him away into the outdoors. On these trips he got a refreshed insight to the priorities in life. He realized while hunting that he could not accomplish what he wanted solely by hard work, grit, and strength. He learned that to nourish his soul he had to be outdoors more. He needed to sit and wait to quell his busy mind, a task difficult for so many. His hunting experience enhanced even more the virtue of patience that served him well in life. It's given him a deeper respect for sportsman and wildlife

Moreover, he harkened back at his ancestors and how they had to hunt to survive. If they were going to eat meat, they had to obtain it for themselves. That feeling of self-reliance was a good feeling. He used his bow and arrow mostly to capture the deer. As soon as he got one, he went home. He took it to his brother in law who knew exactly how to slice it into parts to freeze. His sister Ellen cooked it up for the family and they enjoyed the venison very much except for Jack's son.

In fact, his son would never eat the venison. It turned him off the thoughts of eating deer meat. So, one-night Ann cooked the venison and called them steaks. His son couldn't eat it fast enough. As he grabbed a second one, he said mom "where did you get these steaks, they're delicious" and Ann replied "the butcher market". They never told him the steak was venison.

Jack never went on weeklong hunting trips with his friends during the season since he only had one day off from work and had to get back once again to Ann so she could go shopping. So, like his fishing day he also had to cut the hunting day shorter than he would have liked to. His one day off had to be shared with his wife Ann since she did not drive.

Now, he began to think back on the fun he had going golfing with his boss. Jack was an awesome golfer. He and his boss entered a tournament and came in second. Interestingly, they still reminiscence about their golf tournaments, and the fun they had particpating in those tournaments when they talk with one another.

In fact, Jack learned a lot from playing golf. He learned how to create and hold focus. He had to be focused to improve his game. It took and extreme amount of mental and emotional concentration. Focusing on your goals or keeping your attention on the task at hand however long you need to, is an incredibly positive skill that Jack learned playing golf.

Moreover, problem solving was another skill Jack learned. Who would've thought that problem solving is a skill learned in golf? Well, there are times when you must manipulate your way around the course on a windy day. Or maybe the course is riddled with bunkers and you need to plot out your strategy.

Furthermore, golf has taught Jack that there is always room for improvement. No matter what you are doing in life you can always be better, you can always continue to work and grow to becomes the best version possible. By playing this amazing sport Jack learned how to not only respect himself, but others and the golf course. For example, not stepping in someone's line, being quiet while someone else is hitting, waiting your turn, fixing your ball marks, not driving the golf cart on the tee boxes and greens. He also learned the respect of his fellow competitor and sportsmanship. That has helped him is his career and in his personal life.

Lastly, we can't even count how many times things or situations that occur in golf that makes playing extremely difficult. He'd hit a shot that he felt was so perfect, but the result was awful. At times he'd end up with a bad kick in the fairway that put him in the water. Or he'd a hit a sprinkler head and put him 30 yards over the green. It happened! Unfortunately. But, one of the things he started to learn is that he had to start to accept the things that were out of his control. He learned to accept the uncontrollable.

Truly, it's been years since Jack participated in these three activities that he loves and has a passion for. For the past eight years his entire life revolved around Ann and her stroke. He was in a bad place and felt guilty having fun when his wife was suffering in the nursing home with a stroke. That chapter of his life is over, but of course not forgotten. But now that he's been resurrected from the cave, he knows he must go on and live his life now with joy. He worked hard to get to a place in his life where he could experience being happy and feel fulfilled once again.

In any event, he knows that as he creates his future he wants to volunteer in a homeless shelter. He wants to help people who are defeated, down and out and wants to bring joy, vibrance and enthusiasm to their lives. He was living in defeat when chained in Plato's cave and now wants to help the homeless break their chains of bondage too, for those so inclined to do so. He wants to inoculate them with Ann's warm generous loving spirit so they too can live a life of abundance. He hoped when the corona pandemic toned down, he could get involved in this goal.

After many months Jack is still getting his affairs in place since Ann's death. Getting the affairs in order is a dauting task for Jack. When a spouse dies, handling all the necessary details to settle their estate can be overwhelming. With legal issues to take care of, making funeral arrangements, notifying banks, social security, places of prior employment, obtaining marriage certificates and obtaining death certificates and sharing the news of their death to family and friends is totally overwhelming. Knowing exactly what to do when a loved one dies is not easy. As soon as he gets his financial affairs in place, he will pursue his dreams and goals for creating a new life for himself. He remains hopeful, optimistic and is looking forward to the next chapter in his life that will include fishing, hunting, golf, and volunteering.

Surely, he has put his future in God's hands. He knows He has a plan for him; and knows He will guide his steps along the way in his new journey. Jack is feeling confident all will work out. His loss is very painful. Even thinking about it gives him a knot in his stomach and a lump in his throat. And yet he does desire to shift his energy, mind, and heart towards a different direction. In other words, he is ready to begin to create the life that he wants after his devastating loss. With any loss comes enormous fear, and this fear can cause one to restrict their thoughts and behavior, but he is opening himself up to explore and create a new path.

In closing, losing a spouse is one of the most painful experiences one can be put through. You may feel completely numb, or like you are in shock; the world may pause around you. Losing a loved one changes your entire life, especially when the loved one was also your best friend. You may feel lost and stuck, uncomfortable making even the most minor of decisions. Know that like a cut heals over time, emotional pain heals eventually, too. This is not to say that you won't have scars, but you can certainly live on. Many people experience great loss and, after a time, still find a way to live rich, full, and meaningful lives — and so can Jack. His motto is Never Give up! And Jack will create a life for himself that incorporates his passion, desires and one that brings joy, happiness, and enthusiasm. God Bless Jack!

As Elizabeth Kubler Ross said "the most beautiful people are those who have known defeat, known suffering, known struggle, known loss, and have found their way out of the depths … Beautiful people do not just happen". And Jack is one of those beautiful people who will find his way out of the depths and will find his way to leading a meaningful life filled with joy and happiness.

## *14*

# LESSONS LEARNED FROM JACK

THERE ARE MANY lessons to be learned from Jack' life story filled with adversity and trials, setbacks and heartaches. First, he broke the cycle of abuse from his alcoholic father and then came out of a prolonged grief state when his wife was unexpectedly paralyzed from a stroke and finally coping with the loss of his beloved wife. The following are the numerous lessons Jack has taught us by reading his story.

1. **You Become What You Believe** We learned from Jack's life that to break the cycle of abuse from an alcoholic parent one can benefit from having a mentor who can help you renew your mind by reprograming the thinking. He deleted the negative labels placed on him by his father you're a bum, you'll never make anything out of yourself, you have no talent, you're a loser and replaced them with the labels his coach placed on him you're talented, you're a hard worker, you're strong, you're a great team player, your smart, you have perseverance, you never give up, you're well able. Jack internalized those labels his coach placed on him and went on to be the most faithful,

committed husband and warm loving father. The lesson here is what you play in in your mind will determine what kind of life you live. You become what you believe.

2. **Do Not Go by What You See in Your Circumstances**. Jack was determined not to let his circumstances in the way he was raised impact on his life. He set a new standard and became a barrier breaker. He fired back with the help of his coach and was determined not to be an alcoholic, not to be a womanizer, not to use people for his gain. He saw the light and realized how many gifts he had that were just waiting to be released. He stirred up his gifts into a burning flame and gave his all to his wife, son, and career and created a life of joy, happiness and greatness for his family and employer.

3. **Words You Speak About Yourself Give Life to What You're Saying** We saw firsthand what Jack spoke about himself gave life to what he was saying. He realized that his life would move in the direction of his words. As he said I am strong, I will never give up, I am blessed, I will accomplish my dreams he was prophesying his success and victory to new levels providing a wonderful life for his son and wife. He created a life for his family filled with happiness, rich positive memories, and a life of integrity. The lesson here is that words are like seeds the words you speak about yourself give life to what you're saying. When negative thoughts come to mind never verbalize them.

4. **Our Situation Will Change When We Change**. Jack taught us that we need to be grateful for what we have. It's critical to train our minds to see the good, be grateful for what we have. Life goes so much better when we are grateful and content. When we make this change in our mind to be grateful, joy soon follows. The lesson is that our situation will change when we change.

5. **Let Go of the Wrong People in Your Life.** We saw how Jack let go of the toxic people in his life even though they were

family so he could meet the right people who help him grow, inspire him, and help him to become motivated. Letting go of the wrong people allowed him to move on to a new level of his destiny. The lesson is the only thing keeping us from a new level of destiny is the wrong friendships.

6. **Don't Settle for Mediocrity**. We are created for greatness and are not limited by our ability, education, intellect, or our experience. Quit making excuses for what you can't do. As long as you can't imagine it, as long as you can't see it then its not going to happen for you. The first step in rising above mediocrity and living your full potential is to enlarge your vision. The lesson Jack taught us is to to raise your level of expectancy.

7. **Get Rid of the Guilt**. Shake off the condemnation, quit thinking about what could have or should have been, and get back in the game. Jack shook off the guilt of his wife's condemnation and bad moods after her stroke. He shook off the guilt of having fun because his wife was so miserable. He shook off the broken record thinking why us, why did this happen to us, our life is ruined, we'll never feel joy again, I'm so lonely, life is miserable, my life's savings is being eaten up. He renewed his faith, took back his life and found his passion that was art and writing songs and poems and started feeling joy once again without feeling guilty. He shook off the self-pity and got back in the game and started to dance once again. The lesson here is not to let anyone lay guilt trips on you that sabotage your goals and dreams.

8. **Never Give Up.** He got knocked down a few times and felt as though life has caved in on top of him, but he found the strength to get back up and was determined not to stay down. He was unwavering to work his way out of his numerous problems. He changed his mind set to believe these problems are not going to defeat me, these issues are not going to steal my joy. I am not a victim and God will help open doors for me

to move forward. The lesson is if you fall down get up and try again.

9. **Choices We Make Impact on the Quality of Our Lives.** Jack taught us that the choices we make significantly impact on the quality of our life. He chose to be happy each day, he chose to maintain a positive attitude, he chose to delete negative thoughts, he chose to believe in himself, he chose to strengthen his faith, he chose to pursue his passion of art and song writing. All these choices he made improved the quality of his life. The lesson is that the choices we make shape our future circumstances.

10. **Eliminate the Poisons in Your Life.** He taught us that holding on to and wallowing in self-pity, past resentments, blaming the past for your lot in life, unwilling to forgive, letting bitterness take root contaminate your life. They pollute your heart, and affect your personality, relationships, your self-image and exacerbate the pains of the past. The lesson is not to allow all this negativity to take root can so you can bring back joy, happiness, and peace back into your life.

11. **Importance of Faith.** Jack learned that when life gets tough and situations seem dire and bleak his faith carried him through. His faith replenished abundance in his heart and the spirit. His faith allowed him to focus on positivity and find solutions to resolve his problems so he could move back into a state of abundance. He trained his mind to think abundance and he gravitated toward that. He attracted good things because he expected good things. His faith helped him to believe no challenge is too difficult and the stress, anxiety and fear he was experiencing was minimized because he expected good things to happen. His faith helped him find his purpose in life. His faith was the guiding light that pushed him toward his purpose. The lesson is that faith is as important as the air we breathe, while oxygen nourishes the body, faith nourishes the heart and soul.

Faith, at its core, is deep-rooted in the expectation of good things to come. It goes beyond hope. While much of hope lives in the mind, faith is steeped in the heart and the spirit.

12. **Perseverance.** Despite all the suffering Jack experienced he was a fighter. He was determined no matter how hard life maybe he was going keep going despite the numerous setback's that arose. He showed tenacity and determination as he broke the cycle of abuse. He persevered during Ann's illness and never gave up advocating for her, visiting her every single day for over eight years with no vacations, or respite care. When he was knocked down with financial hardship he got back on his feet and continued. Perseverance for Jack intensified his motivation that not only led him to honoring God and his wife Ann but prepared him for something more down the road. Specifically, it helped him take his life back to live in abundance while still supporting his beloved wife. He kept moving, working, and building a life with joy and happiness .The lesson to learn is the way that we stand up for ourselves and push back against obstacles and challenges ultimately writes our character, and leads us to a more successful life.

13. **Responsibility.** the most important lesson we learned from Jack is that our lives are our responsibility. Taking responsibility for our lives is critical. No one can live our lives for us. We are in charge. Each event in our life is a result of the choice we make. Being responsible is not easy. It takes courage, acceptance, and a realistic view of your circumstances. We saw Jack' demonstration of responsibility in his caring love for his son and wife, his career, his support of Ann when she had her stroke, and in his ability to take back his life and feel alive again. The lesson is that you and only you are responsible for yourself and the things that happen in your life.

14. **Courage.** We learned the true meaning of courage. That is to do something that frightens one. Strength in face of pain and

grief. He showed us how he overcame his fear to act in very courageous manner during his horrible childhood, during the grief of losing the wife he once had to a stroke and all the actions he took escape of the cave that imprisoned him. The lesson is that we need courage to constructively encounter fate, defeat despair, and to heroically find and fulfill our destiny.

15. **What It Takes to Be A Great Husband:** He honored Ann, was faithful to her, never failed to love her, advocated for her in time of need, he supported her and was dependable in taking care of her. He never left her side and remained optimistic to the end. He did everything humanly possible to try to bring joy, happiness, and optimism to her life. He truly personifies the courage, sacrifice, love, respect, and admiration it takes to be a warm, loving husband. He was faithful to his vows:

"*to have and to hold from this day forward, for better or for worse, for richer, for poorer,* **in sickness and in health***, to love and to cherish; from this day forward until death do us part,*" The lesson that Jack taught us is what it means to be a faithful, loving, committed husband.

In summary, all these lessons that Jack taught us are invaluable in how we view and live our lives. He taught us what is important in leading a happy joyful life with peace of mind. He helped us create a future that may be more satisfying. His individual character and spirituality can help us to build good relationships personally and professionally.

Moreover, he challenged us to re-examine how we find our purpose, how to react to difficult situations, how to make decisions, how to think more positively, how to increase our self-confidence, and how to help our overall happiness level. He showed us how life is a continuing learning experience.

Another key point that Jack pointed out to us is that throughout our lives we keep falling and rising. Jack taught us that some of the lessons in life come from experience, yet other lessons are learned by watching others or reading books. But most of all he taught us that many lessons in life can only be learned until we face certain situations in life.

Finally, Jack showed us how the choices we make significantly impact on the quality of our life. The choice is there to be happy each day and to maintain a positive attitude. And the choice to dwell negative matters is there for one to make too. However, choosing to believe in yourself, to strengthen your faith, to pursue your passion, to help others, to stay positive are all choices one can make to improve the quality of one's life, and never give up!

The End

*Appendix A*

# Enrichment Reading

**Caregivers**

McMillan, Susan, PhD, ARNP." Impact of Coping Skills Intervention with Family Caregivers of Hospice Patients with Cancer". *American Cancer Society.* (2005): 214-222.

McMillan, Susan SC, Mahon M." Quality of Life of Primary Caregivers of Hospice Patients with Cancer". *Cancer Practitioner* (1996) :191-198.

McMillan, Susan SC, Mahon M. The Impact of Hospice Services On the Quality of Life of Primary Caregivers". *Oncology Nurse Forum* Vol 21: No.7 (1994):1189-1195.

McMillan, Susan SC, Mahon M." Assessment of Quality of Life in Hospice Patients on Admission and at Week Three. *Cancer Nursing*: 17 (1994):52-60.

Osteen, Joel. <u>The Power of I AM Journal The Words That Will Change your Life Today</u>. New York: Faith Words Hachette Book Group, 2016.

Osteen, Joel. <u>Think Better Live Better A Victorious Life Begins in Your Mind.</u> *New* York: Faith Words Hachette Book Group,2016.

Osteen, Joel. <u>The Power of I AM The Words That Will Change your Life Today</u>. New York: Faith Words Hachette Book Group, 2015.

Osteen, Joel. <u>Your Best Life Is Now 7 Steps To Living At Your Full Potential.</u> Faith Words Hachette Book Group ,2004.

Weitzner MA, McMillan SC. The Caregivers Quality of Life Index-Cancer (CQOL) Scale: Revalidation in a Home Hospice Setting". *Journal Palliative Care* (1999) 15: 13-20.

Weitzner, Michael A., MD, Mc Millan, Susan, RN, PHD and Jacobsen, Paul, B, PHD. "Differences Between Curative and Palliative Cancer Treatment Settings". *Journal of Pain and Symptom* Management Vol.17: No6 (1998) 418-428.

### Domestic Violence

**The National Domestic Violence Hotline**
1-800-799-7233 (SAFE)
www.ndvh.org

**National Dating Abuse Helpline**
1-866-331-9474
www.loveisrespect.org

**National Child Abuse Hotline/Childhelp**
1-800-4-A-CHILD (1-800-422-4453)
www.childhelp.org

**National Sexual Assault Hotline**
1-800-656-4673 (HOPE)
www.rainn.org

**National Center for Victims of Crime**
1-202-467-8700

**National Resource Center on Domestic Violence**
1-800-537-2238
www.nrcdv.org and www.vawnet.org

**Futures Without Violence: The National Health Resource Center on Domestic Violence**
1-888-792-2873
www.futureswithoutviolence.org

**National Center on Domestic Violence, Trauma & Mental Health**
1-312-726-7020 ext. 2011
www.nationalcenterdvtraumamh.org

## CHILDREN

**Childhelp USA/National Child Abuse Hotline**
1-800-422-4453
www.childhelpusa.org

**Children's Defense Fund**
202-628-8787
www.childrensdefense.org

**Child Welfare League of America**
202-638-2952
www.cwla.org

**National Council on Juvenile and Family Court Judges**
Child Protection and Custody/Resource Center on Domestic Violence
1-800-527-3233
www.ncjfcj.org

**ALCOHOLIC RESOURCES**

Al-Anon is a **fellowship group** designed to help people who are affected by a loved one's drinking behavior. The support group is also commonly referred to as the Al-Anon Family Group. Another Al-Anon program, Alateen, specifically helps teens and young adults who have watched family members or friends struggle with an alcohol use disorder (AUD).

Al-Anon - Family Support for Alcoholism - Alcohol Rehab Guide
www.alcoholrehabguide.org/support/al-anon/

**GRIEF RESOURCES**

Fink, Joanne, **When You Lose Someone You Love.** Fox House Publishing. East Petersburg, PA. 2015

Hickman, Martha. **Healing After Loss: Daily Meditations for Working Through Grief.** New York: Harpers Collins Publisher, June 2009

James, John, W. and Freidman, Russell. **The Grief recovery Handbook, 20th Anniversary Edition: The Action program Moving beyond Death, Divorce, and Other Losses including Heath, Career and Faith**. Harpers Collins Publishers. March, 2009

Peterson, Randy, **When You Lose Someone You Love God Will Comfort You.** Publications International, Ltd. Lincolnwood, Illinois. 2007

Roe, Gary. **Comfort for the Grieving Spouse's heart: Hope and Healing After Losing your Partner.** Amazon.com Services LLC, October 2019

**Eldercare Locator**
800-677-1116 (toll-free)
eldercarelocator@n4a.org
https://eldercare.acl.gov

**USA.gov**
844-872-4681 (toll-free)
www.usa.gov

**Well Spouse Association**
800-838-0879 (toll-free)
info@wellspouse.org
www.wellspouse.org

This content is provided by the National Institute on Aging (NIA), part of the National Institutes of Health. NIA scientists and other experts review this content to ensure that it is accurate, authoritative, and up to date.

# About the Authors

Pete Delmonico, Sr. is a talented artist, a prolific song and poem writer. He graduated from Valley Central High School 1961. He was the President of his class in ninth grade. At graduation he received the MVP Award for Baseball as a starting pitcher. He received the prestigious Valley Central High School Outstanding Athletic Alumni Award 2011. He was inducted into the Valley Central Athletic Hall of Fame for Basketball and Baseball, an honor bestowed upon so few extraordinary athletes. Pete had a remarkably successful career with Dupont and Stauffer retired after many years. He worked as a mechanic in the Mechanical Engineering Department in Newburgh, New York.

When he retired, he started a second career and worked at the Interstate Bag Company later named Pro Ampac and supervised 85 employees with expert leadership. He was a stellar team member on a bi-annual golf tournament fund raiser for the Franciscan Friars and his team always finished in first and second place. Pete is member of an International Society composed of worldwide leaders in their field. He loves fishing, hunting, and playing golf. He was a devoted husband to Shirley Delmonico for 56 years and is a loving father to Peter Delmonico, Jr.

Dr. Virginia Nodhturft retired from the Department of Veterans Affairs as the Director of Nursing Education, Tampa Florida after 38 years of service to our veterans. She held Staff Nurse, Nurse Manager, Nurse Educator and Associate Chief Nursing Service for Nursing Education positions over the span of her career.

She received the Mount St. Mary College Alumni Award for her contributions to the Nursing Profession. Moreover, she received the Florida Governor Jeb Bush Sterling Award and the Department of Veterans Affairs National Director's Commendation for Leadership and Excellence for the research she conducted in Managing Multiple Chronic Diseases. Additionally, for her significant contributions to Nursing Education she received the Florida Nurses Association Award and the Nursing Education Association Tampa Award.

Dr. Nodhturft held faculty positions with the University South Florida College of Nursing and University of Tampa College of Nursing. She is a contributor to the nursing literature.

Dr. Nodhturft possesses an Associate Degree in Nursing from Orange County Community College, a Baccalaureate Degree in Nursing from Mount Saint Mary College, Newburgh New York. A Master's Degree in Nursing from New York University, Manhattan, New York, and a Doctorate in Higher Education from Nova University, Ft. Lauderdale, Florida

Interestingly, she is the author of a book entitled ***FWE Lohmann Elizabeth Van Lew's Civil War Spy*** published May 2019.

She is married to Phil Nodhturft, Jr for 50 years and has one son

Phil, III a practicing Attorney in the Tampa Bay Area. She is the proud Grandma to a four-pound Maltese dog named Indy.

The authors would like to hear from you and may be contacted for questions or comments at: ginny3644@verizon.net

CPSIA information can be obtained
at www.ICGtesting.com
Printed in the USA
BVHW060734180121
598042BV00015B/2721